SYMBOLIC COMPUTATION

Artificial Intelligence

Other titles in this series see page 181

Alan Bundy (Ed.)

Catalogue of Artificial Intelligence Techniques

Third, Revised Edition

Springer-Verlag
Berlin Heidelberg New York
London Paris Tokyo
Hong Kong Barcelona

Editor

Alan Bundy
Department of Artificial Intelligence
University of Edinburgh
80 South Bridge, Edinburgh EH1 1HN
Scotland, U.K.
Tel.: (44)-(31)-225 7774 ext. 242

JANET: bundy@uk.ac.edinburgh
ARPANet: bundy@rutgers.edu

Assistant Editor

Alan Smaill

This edition is a completely revised version of the "Catalogue of Artificial Intelligence Tools", 2nd edition, 1986.

ISBN 3-540-52959-4 Springer-Verlag Berlin Heidelberg New York
ISBN 0-387-52959-4 Springer-Verlag New York Berlin Heidelberg

ISBN 3-540-16893-1 Springer-Verlag 2. Auflage Berlin Heidelberg New York
ISBN 0-387-16893-1 Springer-Verlag 2nd Edition New York Berlin Heidelberg

Library of Congress Cataloging-in-Publication Data
Catalogue of artificial intelligence techniques/ Alan Bundy, ed.; assistant editor, Alan Smaill. (Symbolic computation. Artificial intelligence) Rev. ed. of: Catalogue of artificial intelligence tools/edited by Alan Bundy. 2nd rev. ed. c1986. Includes bibliographical references and index.
ISBN 3-540-52959-4 (Springer-Verlag Berlin Heidelberg New York Hong Kong Barcelona)
ISBN 0-387-52959-4 (Springer-Verlag New York Berlin Heidelberg Hong Kong Barcelona)
1. Artificial intelligence - Data processing. I. Bundy, Alan. II. Smaill, Alan. III. Bundy, Alan. Catalogue of artificial intelligence tools. IV. Series. 0336.B86 1990 006.3-dc20
90-46061

2145/3140-543210 - Printed on acid-free paper

Preface

The purpose of the Catalogue of Artificial Intelligence Techniques is to promote interaction between members of the AI community. It does this by announcing the existence of AI techniques, and acting as a pointer into the literature. Thus the AI community will have access to a common, extensional definition of the field, which will promote a common terminology, discourage the reinvention of wheels, and act as a clearing house for ideas and algorithms.

The catalogue is a reference work providing a quick guide to the AI techniques available for different jobs. It is not intended to be a textbook like the Artificial Intelligence Handbook. Intentionally, it only provides a brief description of each technique, with no extended discussion of its historical origin or how it has been used in particular AI programs.

The original version of the catalogue was hastily built in 1983 as part of the UK SERC-DoI, IKBS Architecture Study. It was adopted by the UK Alvey Programme and, during the life of the programme, was both circulated to Alvey grant holders in hard copy form and maintained as an on-line document. A version designed for the international community was published as a paperback by Springer-Verlag. All these versions have undergone constant revision and refinement. Springer-Verlag has agreed to reprint the catalogue at frequent intervals in order to keep it up to date and this is the third edition of their paperback version. We hope that it has now matured into a comprehensive reference book of techniques in Artificial Intelligence.

By 'AI techniques' we mean algorithms, data (knowledge) formalisms, architectures, and methodological techniques, which can be described in a precise, clean way. The catalogue entries are intended to be non-technical and brief, but with a literature reference. The reference might not be the 'classic' one. It will often be to a textbook or survey article. The border between AI and non-AI techniques is fuzzy. Since the catalogue is to promote interaction, some techniques are included because they are vital parts of many AI programs, even though they did not originate in AI.

We have not included in the catalogue separate entries for each slight variation of a technique, nor have we included descriptions of AI programs tied to a particular application, nor of descriptions of work in progress. The catalogue is not intended to be a dictionary of AI terminology, nor to include definitions of AI problems, nor to include descriptions of paradigm examples.

Entries are short (abstract length) descriptions of a technique. They include a title, list of aliases, contributor's name, paragraph of description, and references. The contributor's name is that of the original author of the entry. Only occasionally is the contributor of the entry also the inventor of the technique. The reference is a better guide to the identity of the inventor. Some entries have been subsequently modified by the referees and/or editorial team, and these modifications have not always been checked with the original contributor, so (s)he should not always be held morally responsible, and should never be held legally responsible.

The original version of the catalogue was called "The Catalogue of Artificial Intelligence Tools" and also contained descriptions of portable software, e.g. expert system shells and knowledge representation systems. Unfortunately, we found it impossible to maintain a comprehensive coverage of either all or only the best such software. New systems were being introduced too frequently and it required a major editorial job to discover all of them, to evaluate them and to decide what to include. It would also have required a much more frequent reprinting of the catalogue than either the publishers, editors or readers could afford. Also expert system shells threatened to swamp the other entries. We have, therefore, decided to omit software entries from future editions and rename the catalogue to reflect this. The only exception to this is programming languages, for which we will provide generic entries.

Cross references to other entries in the catalogue are marked < **N** >; where **N** is the reference number of the entry. The entries are listed and numbered in alphabetic order. There are two indices to help you find entries: the 'Logical Table of Contents' lists the entries under various subfields of AI, and the 'Index of Definitions' is a topic/keyword **index**. Both indices refer to the numbers of the entries rather than the numbers of the pages they occur on. Words that appear in the index are in **boldface** in the text.

New entries for the catalogue or suggestions about its organisation or content are welcome, and should be sent to me (see p. iv).

Alan Bundy

Reference

Intelligent Knowledge Based Systems: A Programme for Action in the UK. SERC-DoI, 1983. Available from Mike Wilson, Rutherford Appleton Laboratory, Informatics Division, Didcot, Oxon, OX11 0QX.

Foreword

"... nine words. In English it would take a couple of books full of schematics and electrical and architectural specifications. They have the proper nine words. We don't."

Samuel R. Delany, Babel-17.

This catalogue has both a descriptive and a prescriptive role—it tries to say both what AI is, and what it should be. The descriptive role grew from my beliefs about the nature of AI, and the prescriptive role grew from of my dissatisfaction with the methodology of AI. In brief my views are as follows.

- There is a methodological malaise in AI, the symptoms of which are: (a) differences among referees and critics as to the criteria for judging AI research, (b) the fragility of AI programs, and (c) the difficulty of rebuilding AI programs from published descriptions.
- This malaise can be cured if AI researchers can agree on the nature of AI, on the methodology for pursuing it and on the criteria for assessing it.
- In order to understand the nature of AI it is necessary to separate off computer science, knowledge engineering and cognitive science from basic AI, just as pure mathematics, engineering and physics are separated off from applied mathematics.
- That basic AI is best viewed as: 'the investigation of computational *techniques* which have the potential of exhibiting intelligent behaviour'.

These views are developed more fully in [1].

The core of basic AI consists of the techniques which AI has developed to date. In listing them in this catalogue, I hope we have revealed this core, and thus produced a useful reference work for people in the field. Of course, that is not all there is to AI. Firstly, we have not attempted to go into the details of the techniques, nor even to describe them in an algorithmic manner. We have not described the relations between the techniques, nor their advantages, limitations and history. Secondly, experienced researchers share a common set of benchmark problems, a common methodology and a common set of assessment criteria. These are not described in the catalogue either. We hope that the references we have provided with each technique will serve as a pointer into the literature which will enable the reader to recover this missing information.

But thirdly, we have by no means succeeded in an exhaustive coverage of AI techniques. Part of the blame for this must lie with the editor and review committee for failing to collect all that is available. Part of the blame, however, lies with the methodological malaise mentioned above; the techniques have just not been distilled from the programs in which they were developed. The programs have been described in the 'look ma, no hands' style, i.e. the performance of the program has been described with inadequate explanation or discussion of the techniques which enabled this performance. Even where techniques have been described adequately, the terminological confusion in the field has made it difficult to decide where a new technique is being described with old terminology, and where an old technique is being described with new terminology.

This is where the prescriptive role of the catalogue comes into play. I hope that AI researchers will feel obliged to fit their work into the catalogue, and this will force them to be explicit about the techniques they have invented, improved or tested. I hope that the terminology used in the catalogue will become standard, so that people will stop inventing new terms for old ideas. On the other hand, I hope that the definitions of the old terms in the catalogue will prevent people reusing the old terminology in a new way, and that the authors of the catalogue will be forced to tease apart any different uses of current terms, and rename them. I also hope that researchers will be encouraged to undertake analytic research, investigating the properties of existing techniques, generalizing them, and discovering their interrelations.

In order to play this role it is vital that the catalogue be dynamic, so I am delighted that Springer-Verlag will reprint it periodically. The current edition is the third. Please read through this catalogue with a critical eye, and with the following questions in mind.

- Where would my work fit in here? What techniques have I invented, improved or tested?
- How could this catalogue be improved? Which techniques are missing? Which techniques are poorly explained? Which explanations are faulty or out of date?
- How could these techniques be improved? Which ones could be generalized? Which ones could be made more powerful?
- What aspects of AI research are not captured by this catalogue?

If you have suggestions for improving the catalogue then please send them to me.

The views expressed above are entirely my own, and are not necessarily shared by the members of the review committee or contributors to the catalogue, who had their own grounds for thinking that it was worthwhile to devote time and energy to the catalogue. Whatever their grounds, I am grateful for their efforts.

Reference

Bundy, A. *What kind of field is AI?*, Research Paper 305, Department of Artificial Intelligence, University of Edinburgh, 1986. Also to appear in *Proceedings of the Workshop on the Foundations of Artificial Intelligence*, New Mexico, 1987.

Acknowledgements

I would like to thank the SERC and DoI, who funded the production of this catalogue as part of the Study of Architectures for Intelligent Knowledge-Based Systems; those members of the AI/IKBS community who wrote the individual entries; the review committee of the catalogue; Robin Boswell, Chris Dipple, Carole Douglas, Kave Eshghi, Bob Fisher, John Hallam, Mike Harris, Luis Jenkins, Helen Lowe, Seán Matthews, Mary-Angela Papalaskaris, Dave Plummer, Maarten van Someren, Andrew Stevens, Millie Tupman, and Toby Walsh who did the low level typing/editing work; John Taylor, for setting up the Architecture Study and for his unflagging enthusiasm and encouragement; Bill Sharpe, for being an ever present source of advice, help and information; John W.T. Smith for bearing the burden of the on-line catalogue; Lincoln Wallen, who emerged as the coordinator and editorial assistant in a time of need; and to Alan Smaill who has recently taken over this vital role from Lincoln.

Alan Bundy

Logical Table of Contents

Knowledge Representation

Learning

Logic Programming

Natural Language

Pattern Recognition and Image Processing

Planning

Problem Solving

Theorem Proving

Vision

1 $2\frac{1}{2}$-D Sketch

A viewer-centred representation making explicit the depths, local orientations and discontinuities of visible surfaces, created and maintained from a number of cues e.g. **stereopsis <227>** and **optical flow <162>**. It was thought by Marr to be at the limit of pure perception, i.e. subsequent processes are no longer completely data-driven, and for him it provides a representation of objective physical reality that precedes the decomposition of the scene into objects.

Contributors: T P Pridmore, S R Pollard, S P Stenton.

Reference

Marr, D. *Vision: a computational investigaion into the human representation and processing of visual information.* Freeman, New York, 1982.

2 A* Algorithm

A form of **heuristic search <98>** that tries to find the cheapest path from the initial state to the goal. Its characteristic feature is the **evaluation function**. This is the sum of two components: the estimated minimum cost of a path from the initial state to the current state, and the estimated cost from the current state to the goal. The first component can be calculated if the **search space <226>** is a tree, or it can be approximated by the cheapest known path if the search space is a graph. The second component must be defined, like any evaluation function, with respect to the domain. The heuristic power of this method depends on the properties of the evaluation function.

Contributor: Maarten van Someren.

Reference

Hart, P.E., Nilsson, N.J. and Raphael, B. A formal basis for the heuristic determination of minimum cost paths. *IEEE Transactions on SSC*, 4:100–107, 1968. A correction was published in SIGART Newsletter 37:28-29, 1972.

3 Abduction

Abduction was identified by the philosopher Charles Pierce as an especially important form of hypothesis formation. In the simplest case it has the form: from "A" and "B implies A" infer "B". The abductive hypothesis "B" can be regarded as a possible explanation of "A". To be a useful hypothesis, "B" should be consistent with other beliefs. Abduction is non monotonic and non deterministic. For example, from "A", and "B implies A", and "C implies A" we can infer "B" or we can infer "C" as possible alternative hypotheses. Adding "not B" as a new belief, non monotonically withdraws "B" as a hypothesis. In comparison to this logical view, some researchers like Reggia have taken Peirce's original idea and interpreted it in terms of set coverings. Abduction has recently gained popularity in Artificial Intelligence for such applications as fault diagnosis, language understanding and image understanding. It has also been proposed as an alternative to **non monotonic logics <155>** for **default reasoning <54>**.

Contributor: Robert Kowalski.

References

Charniak, E. and McDermott, D. *Introduction to Artificial Intelligence*, pages 21-22. Addison-Wesley, Reading, Mass., 1985.

Peirce, C.S. in C. Hartshorn et al, editors, *Collected papers of Charles Sanders Peirce*, Volume 2. Harvard University Press, Cambridge, Mass., 1932.

Reggia, J. Diagnostic expert systems based on a set-covering model. *International Journal of Man Machine Studies*, 19(5):437–460, 1983.

4 Actors

The actor model of computation was developed by Hewitt in order to explore the fundamental issues involved with computation via **message-passing**. Actors are objects which know about other actors and can receive messages from other actors. Each actor is specified by detailing what kind of messages it will receive, and the sequence of actions of the actor, should it be sent one of these messages. Everything in an actor based programming system is an actor. To increment a value, for instance, a message would be sent to the actor representing the number, asking the actor to increment itself. The essential difference between the actor model of computation and the **SmallTalk-80** language is that the sequencing of computations by actors depends critically on the concept of a '**continuation**'. A continuation is an actor which is prepared to accept an (intermediate) value as a message, and continue the computation. In SmallTalk-80, an object (or actor) will instead return a message to the object which instigated the computation, in much the same way that a Pascal function will return a value to the routine which called it.

Contributor: Mark Drummond.

Reference

Hewitt, C. Viewing control structures as patterns of passing messages. *Artificial Intelligence*, 8:323–364, 1977.

5 Agenda Based Systems

An **agenda** is a data structure containing tasks to be performed during a problem solving process, which may have attached justifications (for performing that particular task, see **Truth Maintenance Systems <245>**) and/or ratings of importance. Agenda based systems are a means of controlling inference, using some method of adding tasks to the agenda and of selecting, executing, and deleting tasks from the agenda. Tasks may be placed on the agenda simply as they are generated, either directly or as subtasks of existing tasks, with the agenda functioning simply as a stack. Otherwise, the usual control sequence for processing in agenda based systems, assuming tasks on the agenda are sorted by rating (importance), is:

1. Choose the most promising task from the agenda
2. Execute this task
3. If subtasks are generated then
   - if a subtask is already on the agenda then add any new justifications (resulting from the current task) to its list of justifications

if a subtask is not on the agenda, then insert it, together with its justifications

- compute the new ratings for all the tasks on the agenda

4. Re-sort the agenda by rating.

Such systems essentially implement a **Best First Search** strategy with the rating of each node as its heuristic score. Examples of agenda based systems include DENDRAL, AM, CENTAUR, and KRL. **Blackboard Systems <20>** also use agendas to control their operation.

Contributor: Helen Lowe.

Reference

Rich, E. *Artificial Intelligence.* McGraw Hill, New York, 1983.

6 Alpha/Beta Pruning

The minimax procedure **minimax <141>** need not be applied to every branch of the **search tree <226>**. Newell first observed that once a branch of a tree has been refuted, it need not be refuted again. The alpha-beta procedure was first formalised by McCarthy. Its properties are such that it is highly dependant on the order of presentation of alternatives. When alternatives are presented in the best order, it is possible to save $O(n^{\frac{1}{2}})$ of the total effort, where n is the number of leaf nodes in the tree. Recent advances in game searching, such as **Iterative Deepening <118>** and the use of Trans-Ref hash tables, have improved the performance of the alpha-beta search beyond the above specified bound. This is due to the fact that near perfect ordering can be achieved when the tree has many identical nodes in it, but in this case it can be more properly analysed as a graph.

Contributor: Hans Berliner

References

Newell, A., Simon, H. and Shaw, C. Chess playing programs and the problem of complexity. In E.A. Feigenbaum and J. Feldman, editors, *Computers and Thought*, pages 39–70. McGraw-Hill, New York, 1963.

Slagle, J.R. and Dixon, J.K. Experiments with some programs that search game trees. *Journal of the ACM*, 16(2):189–207, April 1969.

Slate, D.J. and Atkin, L.R. Chess 4.5 - the Northwestern University chess program. In P. Frey, editor, *Chess Skill in Man and Machine*, pages 82–118. Springer-Verlag, Berlin, 1977.

7 Analogical Problem Solving

A technique whereby the current problem is solved by retrieving from memory a previously solved similar problem and appropriately adapting that problem's solution. Carbonell has developed a particular version of this technique based on **means/ends analysis <137>**.

Contributor: Jim Doran.

Reference

Carbonell, J.G. A computational model of analogical problem solving. In *Proceedings of IJCAI-81*, pages 147–152. International Joint Conference on Artificial Intelligence, 1981.

8 AND/OR Graphs

Alias: **Game trees.**

AND/OR graphs consist of nodes (representing goals and subgoals) connected by directed links - either AND links (representing subgoals that make up their parent goal) or OR links (representing alternative goals that satisfy the parent goal). AND/OR graphs are often used in theorem provers and game-playing programs. In the latter, moves available to a player from his/her position are given by OR links (representing the possible choices he/she can make) whilst his/her opponent's moves are represented by AND links (as a response has to be considered to each of them).

Contributor: Toby Walsh.

Reference

Nilsson, N.J. *Principles of Artificial Intelligence.* Tioga Pub. Co., Palo Alto, California, 1980.

9 Associative Database

Associative database provides **pattern directed retrieval** <168> by the 'Get Possibilities/Try Next' mechanism. The provision of **context** layers as in **CONNIVER** and **QA4** allows for items to be associated with a value in some particular context.

Contributor: Austin Tate.

10 Augmented Transition Network

Alias: **ATN**.

A representation for grammars developed from simple **finite state transition networks** by allowing (a) recursion and (b) augmentation, i.e. the use of arbitrary tests and actions on arcs, giving full Turing machine power. The use of registers for storing constituents, and the use of tests and actions on register contents allow great flexibility in parsing, and in particular permit the construction of sentence representations quite distinct from the surface text, e.g. deep as opposed to surface syntactic structures. The form of grammar representation is procedurally oriented, but the grammar itself is separated from the interpretive parser, which is **top-down** <243> and usually **depth-first** <61>. ATNs are a popular formalism and can be adapted, for example, to guide parsing by explicit arc ordering. Problems arise with, for example, passing information between subnets, and the treatment of conjunctions.

Contributor: Karen Sparck Jones.

Reference

Woods, W.A. Transition network grammars for natural language analysis. *Communications of the ACM*, 13:591–606, 1970.

11 Auto-epistemic Logic

Auto-epistemic logic is a logic for modelling the beliefs of agents who reflect on their own beliefs. It can express statements such as "If I do not believe that p then q is true". It characterizes the beliefs that an ideally rational agent would be entitled to hold on the basis of such statements. The most distinctive feature of autoepistemic logic is that it is a **non-monotonic logic <155>**: the set of basic beliefs can be modified with time. An agent who takes as a premise "If I do not believe that p, then q is true" and who does not believe that p, will believe that q. If later he were to adopt the premise p as an additional belief then he would no longer be justified in believing that q. See also **Logics of Knowledge and Belief <132>**.

Contributor: Colin Phillips.

Reference

Moore, R.C. Autoepistemic logic. In P. Smets, E.H. Mamdani et al., editors, *Non-standard Logics for Automated reasoning*. Academic Press, London, 1988.

12 B* Algorithm

B* is a **heuristic search** method that can be applied to both adversary and non-adversary problems, but only when the search has an iterative character. It computes the best next step toward the solution on the basis of an evaluation function.

An evaluation function assigns two values to each node, a pessimistic and an optimistic value, (c.f. **minimax <141>**) on the basis of evaluation of the descendants. In non-adversary search this is done according to the following rules:

1 Evaluate the descendants of a node in arbitrary order. If one of the descendants of a node has a pessimistic value greater than the pessimistic value of its parent, then raise the pessimistic value of the parent to the value of this daughter. If a node has an optimistic value that is higher than that of any daughter, than lower it to the maximal optimistic value of its daughters.

2 Terminate when a daughter of the root of the search tree has a pessimistic value that is not lower than the optimistic value of all other daughters. The arc to that daughter is the best step to do.

In the case of adversary search (*eg.* game playing), B* is the same as **Alpha/Beta search <6>**, except that it stops once it has found the best next move. **Heuristic** or **best first search <98>** may be implemented in this manner. B* is claimed to be a good model of the search of chess masters.

Contributor: Maarten van Someren.

Reference

Berliner, H. The B* tree search algorithm: a best-first proof procedure. *Artificial Intelligence*, 12:23–40, 1979.

13 Backwards Search

Alias: **goal-driven** search, **top-down** search, **backwards chaining**.

A **state space <226>** can be searched from the initial state to the goal state, applying **operators <159>** forward (**forward search <82>**); alternatively the state space can be searched from the goal to the initial state applying the operators in reverse (backwards search).

Contributor: Maarten van Someren.

Reference

Barr, A. and Feigenbaum, E.A. (editors). *The Handbook of Artificial Intelligence*, Volume 1. W. Kaufmann, Los Altos, California, 1981.

14 Bandpass Filter

A bandpass filter is one which allows a band of spatial frequencies to pass through it. This band can be described in terms of the value of its peak frequency and its width at half amplitude. See **spatial frequency channels <223>**.

Contributors: T P Pridmore, S R Pollard, S T Stenton.

Reference

Campbell, F.W.C. Sometimes a biologist has to make a noise like a mathematician. *Prog. Bull.*, 15:417–424.

15 Bayesian Inference

Alias: **statistical inference.**

Bayesian inference is one means by which knowledge based systems can reason when uncertainty is involved. Given a set of mutually exclusive hypotheses H_i and an evidence event E, we obtain from an expert estimates of the prior probabilities $P(H_i)$, and the conditional probabilities $P(E|H_i)$. Bayes' Rule then gives the probability of H_i given evidence E:

$$P(H_i|E) = c \cdot P(E|H_i) \cdot P(H)$$

where c is a normalizing constant ensuring that $P(H_i|E)$ sum to unity. In practical problems E may be any subset of the set of all possible evidence events and the hypothesis of interest may be any subset of the set of all possible hypotheses. This tends to require a vast number of conditional probabilities to be calculated.

A solution is provided by techniques based on **bayesian networks** <**16**>. To specify such a network one need only estimate the conditional probabilities of each elementary event E_j given its immediate causes. When the network formed by these cause-effect relationships is loop free, the probability $P(H|E)$ for any subset E of evidence events and any subset H of hypotheses can be calculated by distributed message-passing techniques. When cycles are unavoidable, **tree clustering** and **cycle cutset** techniques <**42**> can be used to compute $P(H|E)$.

An example of the use of Bayesian inference is the **HUGIN** system.

Contributor: Robert Corlett and Judea Peral.

References

Andersen, S.K., Olesen, K.G., Jensen, F.V. and Jensen, F. Hugin - a shell for building bayesian belief universes for expert systems. In *Proceedings of IJCAI-89*, pages 1080–1085. International Joint Conference on Artificial Intelligence, 1989.

Pearl, J. *Probabilistic Reasoning in Intelligence Systems: networks of plausible inference.* Morgan Kaufmann, San Mateo, California, 1988.

16 Bayesian Networks

Alias: **causal networks, influence diagrams**

A bayesian networks is a graphical representation of probabilistic information, which uses directed acyclic graphs, where each node represents an uncertain variable and each link represents direct influence, usually of causal nature. This graphical representation is used to store probabilistic relationships, to control inferences, and to produce explanations.

To define a coherent probability distribution on all variables in the network, we must assess the conditional probabilities relating each variable to its parent variables. If the network formed by these cause-effect relationships is loop free, then inferences from evidence to hypotheses (e.g., finding the best explanation) can be performed in linear time, using message-passing techniques. When loops are unavoidable, **tree clustering** and **cycle cutset** methods **<42>** can be used to facilitate coherent inferences.

Data dependencies in Bayesian networks are identified by a graphical criterion called **d-separation** ("d" denotes directional), which serves to keep messages from spreading to irrelevant areas of the knowledge base. If a set of nodes Z d-separates set X from set Y, then the variables in X are guaranteed to be irrelevant to those in Y, once we know those in Z. The criterion is similar to ordinary separation in undirected graphs, except that paths traversing head-to-head arrows are discounted whenever these arrows have no descendants in the separating set Z.

Contributor: Judea Pearl.

Reference

Pearl, J. *Probabilistic Reasoning in Intelligent Systems: networks of plausible inference.* Morgan Kaufmann, San Mateo, California, 1988.

17 Beam Search

This is a search method in which heuristics are used to prune the search space to a small number of nearly optimal alternatives. This set comprises the "beam", and its members are then searched in parallel. Applications include speech recognition, vision, constraint directed search, and learning.

Contributor: Helen Lowe.

Reference

Oleinick, P. *The implementation and evaluation of parallel algorithms on C.mmp.* PhD thesis, Carnegie Mellon University, Computer Science Department, 1978.

18 Bidirectional Search

In bidirectional search of a **state space** <226>, search proceeds both **backwards** <13> and **forwards** <82>. The program terminates when a common state is reached, since this means that a path has been found from the initial state to the goal state.

Contributor: Maarten van Someren.

Reference

Barr, A. and Feigenbaum, E.A. (editors). *The Handbook of Artificial Intelligence*, Volume 1. W. Kaufmann, Los Altos, California, 1981.

19 Binary and Grey Scale Moments

In computer vision, moments are scalar values that encode some property of the shape or distribution of an object. They are often used as a compact representation of simple binary shapes, because: (1) they are easy to compute (i.e. real-time hardware to compute moments exists) and (2) a few different moments are often sufficient to characterize uniquely a limited set of shapes. It is also possible to calculate functions of the moments that are invariant to translation, rotation and scale changes.

The ij^{th} moment (m_{ij}) of a binary image about the center of mass (x_0, y_0) is given by:

$$m_{ij} = \sum (x_0 - x)^i (y_0 - y)^j.$$

By varying the parameters i and j the resulting moment can yield a number of useful results such as the area and the **eccentricity**. For a grey scale image whose intensity can be expressed as a function, $f(x, y)$ of x and y, the moment m_{ij} is given by:

$$m_{ij} = \sum f(x, y)(x_0 - x)^i (y_0 - y)^j$$

Contributor: H.W. Hughes

Reference

Gonzalez, R.C. and Wintz, P. *Digital Image Processing.* Addison-Wesley, Reading, Mass., 1977.

20 Blackboard

An architectural technique developed principally for continuous reasoning 'real-time' systems. Based on the concept of 'experts' sitting round a blackboard it attempts to co-ordinate the activities of a number of different **Knowledge Sources** (KS) by providing a global database between them, to which partial solutions to the problem under examination are posted.

The Blackboard is divided into a number of abstraction levels, each one containing hypotheses for partial solutions linked to other levels by logical relationships; a Monitor controls access to these hypotheses and inspects any changes in order to notify KSs of those of interest.

Each KS is independent of all others and interfaces externally in a uniform way that is identical across KSs and in which no KS knows which or how many others exist. In general, a KS monitors a level of the Blackboard for conditions for which its knowledge is applicable, it then proposes to process those conditions by placing an item on the **agenda <5>**. The agenda is a list of possible processing events from which the **scheduler** must choose the one most likely to lead to a complete problem solution. This decision making process can be controlled by a static set of rules about problem solving and a dynamic goal structure, which change as the solution progresses, to focus attention in a data-directed fashion. The chosen event is passed for execution to its instantiating KS.

The Blackboard idea has also been extended to a hierarchical model, with differing concepts on different blackboards and knowledge sources 'piping' information between blackboards in the form of expectations, supports, refutations, etc.

Contributors: Martin Bennet, John Lumley.

References

Erman, L.D., Hayes-Roth, F., Lesser, V.R. and Reddy, D.R. The Hearsay II speech understanding system: integrating knowledge to resolve uncertainty. *Computing Surveys*, 12(2), June 1980.

Erman, L.D. and Lesser, V.R. A multi-level organisation for problem solving using many, diverse, cooperating sources of knowledge. In *Proceedings of IJCAI-75*, pages 483–490, International Joint Conference on Artificial Intelligence, 1975.

21 Bottom-up Parsing

Alias: **data-driven parsing**.

In trying to parse a string with a grammar, if one starts with the string and tries to fit it to the grammar, this is **bottom-up** or **data-driven** parsing. For instance with a **context-free grammar** <**45**>, one starts with a token in the string and works up from there on the basis of rules in the grammar which have that token on their right hand side, trying to reduce eventually to the initial symbol.

Contributor: Henry Thompson.

22 Boundary Detection

Alias: **line finding, curve detection.**

The conventional approach to **image segmentation <108>** in early visual processing is **edge detection <71>** followed by boundary detection. Edge detection produces primitive edge elements, possibly with properties of magnitude and/or direction, at places in the image where the edge detection operator has 'fired'. The task of the boundary detection process is to produce a set of boundaries by appropriately connecting up primitive edge elements. There are two main methods:

- **boundary tracking**
- the generalised **Hough transform <105>**

Since a boundary is, by definition, a connected set of edge elements, boundary tracking chooses any edge element and looks for its neighbours, which are then connected to the initial element to form a boundary. This search process is then continually repeated for the elements at the ends of the boundary until some termination criterion is met (such as not being able to find any nearby neighbours). In the Hough technique, each primitive edge element is transformed into a curve in a transform space representing all the possible boundaries the edge element could be part of. The **transform-space** curves produced by edge elements on the same image boundary should all intersect at the same point in transform space, which can be subjected to the inverse transform to characterise the boundary in the image. Originally applicable to straight boundaries only, this method has been generalised to deal with any curve describable in an analytic or tabular form.

Contributor: Bob Beattie.

Reference

Ballard, D.H. and Brown, C.M. *Computer Vision*, chapter 5. Prentice-Hall, Englewood Cliffs, London, 1982.

23 Boyer-Moore Theorem Prover

This is an **automatic theorem proving** program, whose underlying formalism is **recursive function theory**. The system is designed to prove theorems by continuous application of **rewrite rules** <205> and **structural induction**. The key feature of the program is the heuristics it uses to guide the search. In particular, there are powerful heuristics for the automatic use of induction. Some guidance by the user is necessary, by specifying which lemmas must be known before the goal theorem is attempted. Lemmas must be proved by the system before they are automatically used, so the theorem prover is assured of the validity of the proof of the final theorem. The system is not complete, however, since some heuristics generalise the theorem. Its standard set consists of 400 theorems, including the soundness and completeness of a tautology checker for propositional calculus, the equivalence of interpreted and optimised compiled code for a simple arithmetic language, the correctness of a fast string-searching algorithm, the prime-factorization theorem and the unsolvability of the halting problem.

Contributor: Leon Sterling.

Reference

Boyer, R. and Moore, J. *A Computational Logic.* ACM Monograph, Academic Press, New York, 1979.

24 Branch-and-bound Algorithms

A solution technique for **discrete optimisation** problems which is widely used outside AI and is closely related to the **A* Algorithm** <2>. The task is to find the optimally valued tip of a walkable search tree. A subtree of the search tree need not be searched if a computation at its root yields a bound for its set of tip values which implies that none of them can be optimal.

Contributor: Jim Doran.

Reference

Aho, A.V., Hopcroft, J.E. and Ullman, J.D. *Data Structures and Algorithms*, pages 330–336. Addison-Wesley, Reading, Mass., 1983.

25 Breadth-first Parsing

Amounts to **breadth-first searching** <26> of the tree of alternatives which arise in the parsing process. The opposite of **depth-first parsing** <60>.

Contributor: Henry Thompson.

26 Breadth-first Search

An uninformed **graph searching** strategy in which each level is searched before going to the next deeper level. This strategy guarantees finding the shortest path to the node sought first: any path to the solution that is of length n will be found when the search reaches depth n, and this is guaranteed to be before any node of depth greater than n is searched.

Contributor: Dave Plummer.

Reference

Nilsson, N.J. *Principles of Artificial Intelligence*, Tioga Pub. Co., Palo Alto, California, 1980.

27 Caching

Alias: **Infinite recursion, common subgoals.**

When searching a goal tree, an unbounded amount of work can be wasted solving the same problem over and over. Even worse, an unbounded amount of work can be wasted in an infinite recursion. The standard technique of caching previous results can solve both problems. The cache is indexed by goal, normally implemented as a hash table. Each goal is associated with its current solution status - either it is solved (in which case the answer is stored), it has failed, or it is still open. Whenever a goal is to be proved, the cache is searched first. If it is not there, a cache entry marked open should be created. If the cached goal has succeeded or failed just use the stored answer. In the special case of **depth-first search <61>**, infinite recursion occurs when an open cached goal is re-encountered; in this situation, the goal should be treated as though it has failed, though it should not be recorded as such in the cache since an alternative path might still succeed. It also worthwhile canonicalizing the cach entries so that similar goals can be recognised. **Earleys algorithm <70>** is an example of the use of caching.

Contributor: Don Cohen

Reference

Cohen, D. and Mostow, J. Automatic program speedup by deciding what to cache. In *Proceedings of IJCAI-85*, pages 165–172. International Joint Conference on Artificial Intelligence, 1985.

28 Camera Calibration

A technique used to estimate the parameters of the geometric relationship between an image pixel's coordinates and the straight line in the external world along which light traveled to impinge on that pixel. The coefficients depend on both geometry (camera position and orientation) and optics (focal length, image-to-length scale factors, optical center and possible distortions). The standard calibration model assumes linearity (*i.e.* no distortions from a pin-hole model). Under such an assumption, any visible external point with known coordinates determines one of a system of equations describing the relationship of the camera to the world. With enough reference points, the system can be solved for the unknown camera calibration parameters.

Contributor: M. J. L. Orr

Reference

Gremban, K.D., Thorpe, C.E. and Kanade, T. Geometric Camera Calibration using Systems of Linear Equations *IEEE Int. Conf on Robotics and Automation*, 1:562-567, 1988.

29 Cascaded Augmented Transition Network

Alias: **CATN**.

An extension of **augmented transition network** <10> parsing to use a sequence of ordinary ATNs that include among the actions on their arcs a special operation to transmit an element to the next ATN 'machine' in the sequence, with the first machine in the **cascade** taking its input from the input string. Provides a framework for separating e.g. syntactic, semantic and discourse tracking specifications into a cascade of ATNs, one (or more) for each domain. This clean separation of levels of processing means that different higher level partial hypotheses can share the same lower level processing, which in turn can be more flexible due to the loose coupling between the ATN machines (c.f. coupling between subnetworks in an ordinary ATN).

Contributor: John Carroll

Reference

Woods, W.A. Cascaded ATN grammars. *American Journal of Computational Linguistics*, 6:1–12, 1980.

30 Case Frames

A widely used device for the determination and representation of text meaning, based on the organisation of information primarily around verbs, or actions, by **case roles**, e.g. **Agent**, **Instrument**, **Location**. Case frames are usually small-scale structures oriented towards linguistic units like sentences, as opposed to the typical large-scale structures oriented to world knowledge represented by

frames <84>. Though reference to Fillmore's linguistically-motivated ideas is conventional, there is great variation in the treatment of every aspect of case frames, e.g. their relation to features of the **surface text** (is the sentence subject the Agent?), their number (ten or thirty?), their status (obligatory or optional?), the constraints on their fillers (is the Agent HUMAN?), etc. **Conceptual dependency <38>**, for example, uses a small number of deep cases referring primarily to underlying rather than surface relations.

Contributor: Karen Sparck Jones.

Reference

Bruce, B. Case systems for natural language. *Artificial Intelligence*, 6:327–360, 1975.

31 Cellular Arrays

A class of parallel computers consisting of an array of small processors each executing the same instruction on its local data. The processors are often one bit processors (a bit-serial array) and are often arranged in a regular lattice using hexagonal or square tessellation (with or without diagonals). Such arrays are particularly useful for simple image processing where each **image pixel** is generally assigned to a separate processor. Typical examples are **DAP** (from ICL), **CLIP** (from University College London), **MPP** (from Goodyear Aerospace) and **GRID** (from GEC). See **propagation in cellular arrays <188>**.

Contributor: Dave Reynolds.

Reference

Danielsson, P.E. and Levialdi, S. Computer architectures for pictorial information systems. *Computer*, 14(11):53–67, November 1981.

32 Certainty Factors

Certainty factors are used in **production rule systems <184>**, such as **MYCIN**, to express and propagate degrees of belief. They are numbers in the range $[-1, +1]$, $+1$ indicates certainty; -1 indicates impossibility. Measures of belief and disbelief are collected separately and combined by subtracting the latter from the former. Certainty factors are updated to take into account fresh evidence, the laws of combination differing from **Bayesian Inference <15>** in that they are truth functional – the certainty of a formula is a unique function of the certainty of its subformulae. Approximate probabilistic interpretation of certainty factors can be given in term of the likelihood ratio

$$L = \frac{P(e|h)}{P(e|\neg h)}$$

and the transformation,

$$CF = \frac{(L-1)}{(L+1)}$$

The certainty-factor propagation method would produce coherent belief updates if no two rules emanate from the same premise.

Contributor: Helen Lowe.

Reference

Heckerman, D. Probabilistic interretations for MYCIN's certainty factors. In L.N. Kanal and J.F. Lemmer, editors, *Uncertainty in Artificial Intelligence.* North Holland, Amsterdam and Oxford, 1986.

33 Chart Parsing

Chart parsing is an approach to **non-deterministic parsing** developed by Kay and Kaplan based on earlier work by Earley, Kay and Colmerauer. In contrast to that earlier work, in which the **chart** was a (in some cases enriched) **well-formed substring table** for recording intermediate results, the later systems use the chart as the active agent in the parsing process.

The chart is a directed graph, with two sorts of edges - active and inactive. Inactive edges record the existence of complete constituents. Active edges record hypothesised *in*complete constituents. The parsing process itself consists of adding new edges in response to the meeting of active with inactive edges. As a record of an incomplete constituent, an active edge must carry some indication of how it may be extended, e.g. a dotted **context-free rule** or a state in a **network grammar** (**RTN** or **ATN** <**10**>). When an **active edge** and an **inactive edge** meet for the first time, if the inactive edge satisfies the active edge's conditions for extension, then a new edge will be constructed.

If initial hypotheses about constituents are keyed by active edges and their needs, parsing will be **top-down** <**243**>. If on the other hand these hypotheses are keyed by inactive edges, parsing will be **bottom-up** <**21**>. One of the principal advantages of the chart parsing methodology is that it easily supports a variety of grammatical formalisms, rule invocation strategies, and control regimes. See (Thompson and Ritchie 1983) for an elementary introduction, and (Kay 1980) for a detailed theoretical analysis.

Contributor: Henry Thompson.

References

Thompson, H.S. and Ritchie, G.D. Techniques for parsing natural language: two examples. In *Artificial Intelligence Skills*, Harper and Row, 1983. Also available as Research Paper 183, Department of Artificial Intelligence, University of Edinburgh.

Kay, M. Algorithm schemata and data structures in syntactic processing. In *Text Processing: Text Analysis and Generation, Text Typology and Attribution*, proceedings of the Nobel Symposium 51, pages 327–358. Almqvist and Wiksell, Stockholm, 1982. Also available as CSL-80-12, Xerox PARC, Palo Alto, CA.

34 Circumscription

Circumscription captures the idea of "jumping to conclusions", namely that the objects that can be shown to have a certain property are all the objects that satisfy that property. For example, in the missionaries and cannibals problem, we are told that three missionaries and three cannibals want to cross the river in a two-person boat such that the cannibals never outnumber the missionaries in the boat or on either bank. We assume that there are no more cannibals around; the three mentioned in the problem are all there are. More generally, we conjecture that the tuples $\langle x, y, ..., z\rangle$ that can be shown to satisfy a relation $P(x, y, ..., z)$ are all the tuples satisfying this relation. Thus we *circumscribe* the set of all relevant tuples.

Circumscription is a formalised rule of conjecture. **Domain circumscription** (also known as **minimal inference**) conjectures that the known entities are all there are. **Predicate circumscription** assumes that entities satisfy a given predicate only if they have to on the basis of a collection of known facts; since this collection can be added to subsequently. Circumscription together with first order logic allows a form of **non-monotonic reasoning <155>**. Suppose $A(P)$ is a sentence of first order logic containing a predicate symbol $P(\underline{x})$, where $\underline{x} = x_1, x_2, \ldots, x_n$, and that $A(\Phi)$ is the result of replacing all occurrences of P in A by the predicate expression Φ. Then the predicate *circumscription* of P in $A(P)$ is the schema:

$$A(\Phi) \wedge \forall \underline{x}(\Phi(\underline{x}) \rightarrow P(\underline{x})) \rightarrow \forall \underline{x}.(P(\underline{x}) \rightarrow \Phi(\underline{x}))$$

The sentences that follow from the predicate circumscription of a theory are those which are true in all the **minimal models** of that theory.

Contributor: Helen Lowe.

Reference

McCarthy, J. Circumscription - a form of non-monotonic reasoning. *Artificial Intelligence*, 13:27–39, 1980.

35 Classification

Alias: **ID3**.

A **discrimination net <65>** can be built from a set of classified items. The set is repeatedly split into subsets by the value of a predicate, until each subset contains members of one class only. The series of splits defines the **discrimination net**.

To increase the efficiency of the resulting discrimination net, the predicates on which the items are split are chosen using information theoretic techniques so that they make the number of instances in each subset as similar as possible. This technique has been successfully applied to the problem of classifying chess positions as won or drawn.

Contributor: Maarten Van Someren.

Reference

Quinlan, J.R. Discovering rules by induction from large collections of examples. In D. Michie, editor, *Expert systems in the Micro-electronic Age*, pages 168–201. Edinburgh University Press, Edinburgh, 1979.

36 Clausal Form

A normal form for **predicate calculus** <180> formulae borrowed from **mathematical logic**, and much used in **automatic theorem proving**. It consists of applying **prenex normal form**, **skolemization** <222> and **conjunctive normal form**, in succession. The resulting formula has a model if and only if the original formula does. A formula in clausal form consists of a conjunction of clauses. Each **clause** is a disjunction of literals. Each **literal** is either an **atomic sentence** or the negation of an atomic sentence, where an atomic sentence is a predicate applied to some terms.

Horn clauses are a very important subclass of clausal form formulas. They have at most one unnegated literal. Using the **Kowalski form** (where $\neg P_1 \vee \ldots \vee \neg P_m \vee Q_1 \vee \ldots \vee Q_n$ is written as $P_1\&\ldots\&P_m \rightarrow Q_1 \vee \ldots \vee Q_n$) they are formulas of the form:

$$\mathrm{P}_1 \ \& \ \mathrm{P}_2 \ \& \ \ldots \ \& \ \mathrm{P}_n \ \rightarrow \ \mathrm{Q} \qquad \text{or} \qquad \mathrm{P}_1 \ \& \ \mathrm{P}_2 \ \& \ \ldots \ \& \ \mathrm{P}_n \ \rightarrow$$

where each of the P_i and Q are atomic sentences.

Horn clauses have several important properties when viewed from mathematical logic. In addition, they form the basis for the **logic programming** language **Prolog <187>**: each predicate in a Prolog program has a horn clause definition. The above formulae would be written

$$Q \quad :- \quad \mathrm{P1}, \mathrm{P2}, \ldots, \mathrm{Pn}. \qquad \text{and} \quad ?- \quad \mathrm{P1}, \mathrm{P2}, \ldots, \mathrm{Pn}.$$

respectively as Prolog programs.

Contributor: Alan Bundy and Martin Merry.

References

Chang, C. and Lee, R.C. *Symbolic Logic and Mechanical Theorem Proving.* Academic Press, New York, 1973.

Kowalski, R.A. *Logic for problem solving.* North-Holland, New York, 1979.

Chang, C.C. and Keisler, H.J. *Model Theory.* North-Holland, New York, 1973.

37 Computer Audiometry

This technique provides a means for plotting an **audiogram** (given a graphics capability). The algorithm evaluates a person's threshold of hearing by playing a sequence of tones at various frequencies and amplitudes (using a programmable tone generator). The person simply has to answer 'yes' or 'no' with one of two push buttons, as to whether or not he/she can hear the tone; the amplitude decreases until he just can not hear it, otherwise the amplitude increases until he just can hear it. A range of frequencies is tested by playing the tones in ascending octaves, and then in descending octaves and averaging out the results. The audiogram is then plotted on a graphics terminal.

Contributor: Peter Mitchell.

38 Conceptual Dependency

A theory of meaning representation developed by Schank and extensively exploited at Yale, relying on deep 'conceptual' **semantic primitives <214>**

and **case frames** <30> and providing a strong decomposition of word and text meaning. The emphasis on key **primitive acts** and required properties of the fillers of their (obligatory) roles is used to drive primarily **semantic expectation-based parsing**.

Contributor: Karen Sparck Jones.

Reference

Schank R.C. (editor). *Conceptual Information Processing*. North-Holland, Amsterdam and Oxford, 1975.

39 Connection Calculus

Alias: **Clause graph resolution, Connection Graph.**

The **connection calculus** is a proof system for first-order classical **Predicate Calculus** <180> based on the notion of a matrix. The method is due to Wolfgang Bibel (1981) and grew out of an analysis of more standard sequent and tableau methods. A similar method of "matings" was developed independently by Peter Andrews [Andrews 1981].

A formula or entailment of the first-order predicate calculus can be displayed as a (nested) two-dimensional **matrix**. For example, the entailment $A \rightarrow B, B \rightarrow C \ \vdash \ A \rightarrow C$, is represented as the matrix:

$$\begin{pmatrix} A \\ \overline{B} \end{pmatrix} \quad \begin{pmatrix} B \\ \overline{C} \end{pmatrix} \quad \begin{pmatrix} \overline{A} & C \end{pmatrix}$$

where $\overline{A}$ indicates that the occurrence of A is negative, i.e. inside an odd number of explicit or implicit negation signs. The matrix is made up of three columns, the first two of which themselves are matrices with one column and two rows. The third matrix has two columns and one row. Ignoring the brackets and reading horizontal separation as conjunction and vertical separation as disjunction we have the **conjunctive normal form** of the original entailment. (We could just as easily work with the **disjunctive normal form** by attempting to **refute** the entailment rather than prove it.) The **paths** through this matrix are lists of **literals** that contain exactly one element from each column of the matrix, and a **connection** is a pair of literals on a path that are **complementary** (i.e. identical atoms but complements with respect to negation). In our example, $A, \bar{C}, \bar{A}$ is one path, $A, \bar{C}, C$ another. $A, \bar{A}$ and $C, \bar{C}$ are connections on these paths.

The basic characterisation of consequence (or validity) on which the connection calculus rests is that an entailment $\Gamma \vdash A$ holds (i.e. A is a logical consequence of the formulae of Γ) if and only if every path through the matrix representation of the entailment contains a complementary connection. This is a version of Gentzen's Hauptsatz for the logic. In our example, the connections $A, \bar{A}$, $B, \bar{B}$ and $C, \bar{C}$ are said to **span** the matrix because every path through it contains a connection from this (three element) set of connections. The entailment therefore holds. Various so-called **path-checking** algorithms have been designed that simulate resolution strategies, and to take extra advantage of the form of the matrix (see Bibel 1982). In the presence of quantifiers complementarity of connections is calculated by a unification algorithm as in standard **resolution <204>**. The method extends to classical type theory [Andrews 81] and non-classical logics [Wallen 1989].

Contributor: Lincoln Wallen.

References

Andrews, P.B. Theorem proving via general matings. *JACM*, 28(2):193–214, 1981.

Bibel, W. On matrices with connections. *JACM*, 28(4):633–645, 1981.

Bibel, W. *Automated Theorem Proving.* Vieweg, Braunschweig Wiesbaden, 1982 (revised 1987).

Wallen, L.A. *Automated deduction in non-classical logics.* MIT Press, Cambridge, Mass. and London, 1990.

40 Connectionism

The essence of connectionism is that neurons in the brain compute, not by transmitting large amount of symbolic information, but by being appropriately connected to large numbers of similar units. Hence connectionist theories emphasize the design of special purpose parallel architectures to implement computational theories of psychological processes. These architectures are networks of computationally simple units. The operation of a given network depends upon the pattern of connectivity between its component units. The **DADO** machine is an example of a connectionist architecture, consisting of a large number (around a hundred thousand) of processing elements, each comprising its own processor, a small amount of local RAM, and a specialised I/O switch, interconnected to form a complete binary tree. The DADO is designed to provide highly significant performance improvements in the execution of large **production rule system <184>**.

Contributors: T P Pridmore, S R Pollard, S P Stenton.

References

Feldman, J. and Ballard, D. *Computing with Connections.* Technical Report 72, University of Rochester, Computer Science Dept., New York, 1981.

Stolfo, J.S. and Shaw, D.E. Dado: a tree-structured machine architecture architecture for production systems. In *Proceedings of AAAI-82*, pages 242–246, American Association of Artificial Intelligence, 1982.

41 Constituent Likelihood Grammar

Natural language analysis techniques based on generative grammars normally make a sharp distinction between grammatical and ungrammatical sequences and thus fail when exposed to authentic discourse. **Probabilistic techniques** for (a) syntactic category assignment and (b) syntactic structure determination use only the relative frequency of constructions and so do not rule anything out as ungrammatical. The CLAWS system developed at Lancaster University for word tagging using tag pair transition frequencies derived from a large, heterogeneous text corpus achieves 95-96% accuracy.

Contributors: Geoffrey Sampson, Karen Sparck Jones

Reference

Atwell, E. S. Constituent-likelihood grammar. In R. Garside, G. Sampson and G. Leech, editors, *The Computational Analysis of English: a corpus-based approach*, pages 57–65. Longman, London, 1987.

42 Constraint Networks

Constraint networks offer a graphical representation of **constraint satisfaction** problems <**43**> that can be used to control search efficiently. A constraint network is a graph (or hypergraph) in which nodes represent variables and arcs represent pairs (or sets) of variables which are included in a common constraint. The topology of this network uncovers opportunities for problem decomposition techniques and provides estimates of the problem complexity prior to actually performing the search. The following are typical network-based techniques.

- **Cycle Cutset** is a method based on preferentially instantiating variables which intercept cycles in the constraint graph. Once all cycles are intercepted, the rest of the problem becomes tree-structured and can be solved in linear time. The complexity of this scheme is exponential in the size of the cutset found.
- **Adaptive Consistency** is a method based on enforcing local consistency with adjustable scope. Variables are called sequentially, and local consistency is enforced recursively among their uncalled neighbours. Each such operation would normally result in connecting the neighbours with extra links, called "induced constraints". When all variables are called, a backtrack free solution can be found by instantiating the variables in the reverse order.
- **Tree Clustering** is a method of systematic regrouping constraints into hierarchical structures capable of supporting search without backtracking. The complexity of this transformation is exponential in the size of the largest cluster generated and its main advantage is that, once the clusters are structured, queries can be answered in linear time.

Other graph-based techniques include **backjumping**, an improvement on backtracking where, at a dead-end situation, the algorithm retracts to the most recent node connected to the dead-end variable (also see **Dependency Directed**

Backtracking <59>), and decomposition to a tree of connected components where the connected components in the constraint graph are solved first and an overall solution is assembled using a linear tree algorithm.

Contributor: Rina Dechter.

References

Dechter, R. Enhancement schemes for constraint processing: backjumping, learning, and cutset decomposition. *Artificial Intelligence*, 43, February 1990.

Dechter, R. and Pearl, J. Tree clustering for constraint networks. *Artificial Intelligence*, 33:353–366, 1989.

Freuder, E.C. A sufficient condition for backtrack-bound search. *JACM*, 32(4):755–761, 1985.

43 Constraint Satisfaction and Propagation

Alias: **consistent-labeling, satisfaction assignment, CSP**.

Constraint satisfaction is a class of problems in which knowledge is expressed declaratively as a collection of explicit, categorical constraints over a set of possibilities. These include, for example, scene labeling, scene matching, space planning problems, data-base consistency-maintenance, query-answering, Graph Isomorphism detection, the Graph Colouring problem, and many puzzles such as crypto-arithmetic.

The **Constraint-Satisfaction Problem** consists of a set of n variables, $V_1 \ldots V_n$, each represented by its domain values (not necessarily numerical), $D_1 \ldots D_n$, and a set of constraints. A constraint $C_i(V_{i_1}, \ldots V_{i_j})$ is a subset of the Cartesian product $D_{i_1} \times \ldots \times D_{i_j}$ that specifies which values of the variables are compatible with each other. A solution is an assignment of values to all the variables which simultaneously satisfy all the constraints, and the most common task associated with these problems is to find one or all solutions. In practice, the constraints may be specified either as truth-tables, or as lists of the satisfying tuples or, more concisely, in analytic form as expressions (such as $V + V^5 \leq 9$) in some "constraint languages", algebraic or otherwise. See also the entry on **Relaxation Labeling <203>**.

The common algorithm for solving CSPs is the **Backtrack** search algorithm. In its primitive version, called **chronological backtracking**, the algorithm traverses the variables in a predetermined order, provisionally assigning consistent values to a subsequence $(V_1, ..., V_i)$ of variables and attempting to append to it a new instantiation of V_{i+1} such that the whole set is consistent. If no consistent assignment can be found for the next variable V_{i+1}, a dead-end situation occurs, the algorithm "backtracks" to the most recent variable, changes its assignment and continues from there. Chronological backtracking suffers from many maladies and several cures have been offered and analysed in the AI literature. These can be classified into **look-ahead schemes**, and **look-back schemes**. The former are concerned with the decision of what variable to instantiate (e.g. dynamic search rearrangement, max-cardinality search, minimum width), or what value to assign next among all the consistent choices available (e.g. forward-checking, full-lookahead, partial look-ahead, constraint propagation). Look-back schemes concern the decision of where and how to backtrack in case of a dead-end situation. The two fundamental ideas in look-back schemes are **go-back to source of failure**, and constraint recording or learning. The former detect and change decisions that caused the dead-end while skipping irrelevant decisions (e.g. selective backtracking, backjumping), while constraint-recording schemes identify the conflict-sets representing the reasons for the dead-end and record them as explicit constraints to disable the same conflicts from occurring in the future (e.g. **Dependency Directed Backtracking** <59>).

Contributors: Rina Dechter.

Reference

Stefik, M.J. Planning with constraints (Molgen: part 1). *Artificial Intelligence*, 16:111–139, 1981.

44 Constructive Solid Geometry

Alias: **CSG**.

Constructive solid geometry is the **volumetric representation** of objects using compositions of simple solids. Usually the solids are simple cuboids, cylinders, cones or spheres with an arbitrary scale. These undergo rigid transformations in space before being combined using the set operations. Complex shapes are constructed by combining the basic solids using the AND and OR operations while vacancies or holes are formed using the NOT operation to 'bore out' the required shape. These operations reflect the way in which the object being modelled was originally constructed. See also **Generalised Cylinders <90>** and **Superquadrics <234>**.

Contributor: H.W. Hughes

Reference

Voelcker, H.B. and Requicha, A.A.G. Geometric Modeling of Mechanical Parts and Processes. *Computer*, 10:48–57, December 1977.

45 Context-free Grammar

A context-free grammar is a collection of context-free **phrase structure rules**. Each such rule names a constituent type and specifies a possible expansion thereof. The standard notation is:

$$\text{LHS} \rightarrow \text{RHS}_1 \ldots \text{RHS}_n$$

where LHS names the constituent, and RHS_1 through RHS_n the expansion. Such rules are **context-free rules** because the expansion is unconditional - the environment of the constituent to be expanded is irrelevant.

A collection of such rules together with an initial symbol, usually S, is a context-free grammar. The constituents expanded (those appearing on the left hand side) are called the **non-terminals**. Those not expanded (appearing only on the right hand side) are called the **terminals**. There are two standard ways of interpreting such a grammar as specifying a language. The **rewriting interpretation** says that a grammar generates the set of strings of terminals which can be produced by the following non-deterministic method:

1 Write down the initial symbol;

2 Choose a non-terminal symbol in the string, and a rule from the grammar which expands it. Replace one instance of the non-terminal with the expansion given in the rule;

3 If no non-terminals remain in the string, the process is complete. Otherwise, go back to step 2.

The **well-formedness** interpretation actually generates trees, not strings. It simply admits to the language all singly rooted trees whose root is the initial symbol and for each of whose non-leaf nodes there is a rule in the grammar such that *LHS* is the node label and RHS_n are the labels of its descendants in order.

Contributor: Henry Thompson.

Reference

Gazdar, G. Phrase structure grammar. In P. Jacobson and G.K. Pullum, editors, *The Nature of Syntactic Representations*, pages 131–186. Reidel, Dordrecht, 1981.

46 Contour Generator

A Contour Generator is a set of points on a generating object surface that projects to an **occluding contour** in an image. A special case of a contour generator is an extremal boundary of an object, this is a boundary along which a surface turns smoothly away from the viewer. At extremal boundaries the surface normal is perpendicular to both the line of sight and the occluding contour projected into the image.

Contributors: T P Pridmore, S R Pollard, S T Stenton.

References

Barrow, H.G. and Tenenbaum, J.M. Interpreting line drawings as three-dimensional scenes. *Artificial Intelligence*, 17:75–116, 1981.

Marr, D. Analysis of occluding contour. *Proc. Roy. Soc. Lond.*, B197:441–475, 1977.

47 Contradiction Backtracing

A method to discover and correct faulty hypotheses in a theory. If a proposition that is derived from a set of hypotheses turns out to be false in terms of a **model**, the derivation can be used to identify the faulty hypotheses. Contradiction backtracing uses the trace of a **resolution <204>** proof, in which the false proposition was the goal. The proof is traced backwards from the empty clause. Each clause is **semantically evaluated** by the user or in a standard model. If it is false, the negated parent clause is considered next, and otherwise the positive parent. The substitutions that allowed the resolution steps are accumulated and applied to each following clause. The procedure will finally lead to a hypothesis which is false.

Contributor: Maarten van Someren.

Reference

Shapiro, E.Y. An algorithm that infers theories from facts. In *Proceedings of IJCAI-81*, pages 446–451. International Joint Conference on Artificial Intelligence, 1981.

48 Contrast Sensitivity Function

The contrast sensitivity function is a normalised description of a system's sensitivity to spatial frequencies in terms of the contrast required to perform some perceptual task. For detection tasks, the human C.S.F. peaks at around 3-5 cycles/deg and reaches zero at about 60 cycles/deg. See **modulation transfer function <145>**.

Contributors: T P Pridmore, S R Pollard, S T Stenton.

Reference

Wilson, H.R. and Giese, S.C. Threshold visibility of frequence gradient patterns. *Vision Research*, 17:1177–1190, 1977.

49 Convolution

The application of a mathematical operation to each neighbourhood in an image is called convolution. The operation is defined by a 'mask' specifying for each neighbourhood, how many points it contains and how the corresponding image point affects the computations. Each location in the operator mask contains a weighting value, these are multiplied by the value of the corresponding image location and the results summed to give the convolution value for that neighbourhood. Doing this for all neighbourhoods produces a new array of values. Mathematically, the convolution integral is the integrated cross product of a weighting function with an image. See **local grey-level operations <130>**.

Contributors: T P Pridmore, S R Pollard, S T Stenton.

Reference

Frisby, J.P. *Seeing: illusion, brain, and mind.* Oxford University Press, Oxford, England, 1979.

50 Curvature Maps

The representation of the curvatures of an image considered as a surface - usually applied to depth maps. The normal curvature of a surface at a point reaches its maximum and minimum, the **principal curvatures**, at directions in the surface which are perpendicular. At an **umbilic point**, *e.g.* on a plane or sphere, the normal curvature is independent of direction. The **Gaussian curvature** (frequently denoted K), the product of the principal curvatures, and the **mean curvature** (frequently denoted H), the mean of the principal curvatures, may be used to classify the surface type into perceptually significant categories according to their sign.

Contributor: R.M. Cameron-Jones

Reference

Besl, P. and Jain, R. Intrinsic and Extrinsic Surface Characteristics. *IEEE CS Conference on Computer Vision and Pattern Recognition*, pages 226–233, 1985.

51 Data-directed Control

Alias: **data-driven control, bottom-up, forward chaining.**

A technique for interpretation or evaluation of a set of clauses which represent constraints or equations on unknown data items. The evaluation proceeds in pseudo-parallel **breadth-first search <26>** fashion starting with those predicates where enough data items have values. These compute values which are then used in other clauses which are added to a queue for evaluation. Evaluation proceeds until no more predicates can be evaluated. Evaluation of some predicates may generate other clauses, in which case care must be taken to avoid an explosion of partially evaluated clauses. Control depends not on the initial order of the clauses, but on the order in which data items get their value. **Demons <57>** can be used to implement data-directed control.

Contributor: P.M.D. Gray.

Reference

Elcock, E.W., McGregor, J.J. and Murray, A.M. Data directed control and operating systems. *The Computer Journal*, 15(2):125–129, May 1972.

52 Decision Theory

Decision Theory provides a basis for making choices in the face of uncertainty, based on the assignment of probabilities and payoffs to all possible outcomes of each decision. The space of possible actions and states of the world is represented by a **decision tree**, whose nodes may be

1. decision nodes (actions which may be performed by the user)
2. chance nodes (events over which the user has no control, with associated probabilities)
3. terminal nodes (outcomes) to which utilities are attached.

The decision tree is evaluated by calculating the expectation of the utility at each chance node and applying the maximisation operator at each decision node. The decision tree can be generated automatically from more economical representations of the decision environment such as influence diagrams or **Bayesian Networks** <**16**>. Other methods for dealing with uncertainty are **Bayesian Inference** <**15**>, **Dempster-Shafer Theory** <**58**> and **Certainty Factors** <**32**>.

Contributor: Helen Lowe.

Reference

Pearl, J. *Probabilistic Reasoning in Intelligence Systems: networks of plausible inference.* Morgan Kaufmann, San Mateo, California, 1988.

53 Deductive Program Synthesis

Alias: extracting answers from proofs

Program synthesis is the derivation of a program to meet a given specification. According to the deductive approach, program synthesis is regarded as a theorem-proving task. The system proves the existence of an output that satisfies the specification. This proof is restricted to be constructive in the sense that it must indicate a computational method of finding the output. This method becomes the basis for a program that is extracted from the proof.

Contributor: Richard Waldinger.

Reference

Manna Z. and Waldinger R. *The Logical Basis for Computer Programming*, Volume 1. Addison-Wesley, Reading, Mass. and London, 1985.

54 Default Logic

Alias: **Default Reasoning**

In reasoning about incompletely specified worlds, it may be necessary to make default assumptions that lead to tentative conclusions. For example, if we know that Tweety is a bird, we may assume that Tweety can fly. If we later discover that Tweety is an ostrich, we may retract this assumption. Hence inferences based on such assumptions may need to be modified or rejected on the basis of later revelations. One way of accounting for default reasoning is through non-monotonic logic (see **non-monotonic reasoning <155>**), which allows conclusions to be rejected when more information is added to the premises. In non-monotonic logics, the usual set of axioms used in deriving theorems is augmented by a set of default rules which serve to infer conclusions that cannot otherwise be derived.

Formally, a default logic is a pair (W, D), where W is a set of first-order sentences and D is a set of default rules, each of which has the form

$$\frac{a : b}{c}$$

which can be read as "from a and the inability to prove $\neg$b, infer c". The first order sentences a, b, and c are called the prerequisite, the justification, and the consequent of the default, respectively. The defaults can be viewed as extending the knowledge (as contained in W) that we have about the world. Any acceptable set of beliefs about that world is called an "extension". Default theories may have none, exactly one, or many extensions.

Contributor: Helen Lowe.

Reference

Reiter, R. A Logic for Default Reasoning. *Artificial Intelligence*, 13:81–132, 1980.

55 Definite Clause Grammars

A DCG consists of a set of rules in a notation based on **Logic Programming <131>**. Each rule is similar to a **context-free rule <45>**, with variables to show connections between the constituents involved, and an arbitrary test or action can be appended to the rule (for example, to handle number-agreement). DCGs are an extension of the grammar-rule notation in **Prolog <187>**, and can be used to parse a string simply by interpreting them in a manner similar to the execution of a Prolog program.

Contributor: Graeme Ritchie.

Reference

Pereira, F. and Warren, D.H.D. Definite clause grammars for language analysis - a survey of the formalism and a comparison with augmented transition networks. *Artificial Intelligence*, 13:231–278, 1980.

56 Delayed Evaluation

A technique for generating a piece of program as a sequence of instructions (or as a composition of functions) from a set of clauses which specify constraints on data items. The data items are represented by tokens some of which are replaced by list structures representing 'recipes' or promises to construct the given items from other items. The clauses are run through an interpreter using **data-directed control <51>** which 'evaluates' the predicates. Instead of producing the computed result it gives a composed function or 'recipe' which can be translated into a sequence of instructions to compute the result. This technique can also be combined with **partial evaluation <165>**. The technique can also be used with a procedural program to delay the evaluation of certain calls e.g. for database or data-structure access, until a statement to print the result is encountered. In the context of **applicative languages <87>** this technique is known as **lazy evaluation <123>**.

Contributor: P.M.D. Gray.

References

Gray, P.M.D. *Compiling Programs from Problem Descriptions.* Research Report, Dept. of Computing Science, University of Aberdeen, 1970.

Todd, S.J.P. The peterlee relational test vehicle. *IBM Systems Journal*, 15:304, 1976.

57 Demon

Alias: **antecedent theorem, if-added** method.

A portion of a program which is not invoked explicitly, but which lies dormant waiting for some condition(s) to occur. For example, a knowledge manipulation program might implement **inference rules** as demons. Whenever a new piece of knowledge was added, various demons would activate (which demons depends on the particular piece of data) and would create additional pieces of knowledge by applying their respective inference rules to the original piece. These new pieces could in turn activate more demons as the inferences filtered down through chains of logic. Meanwhile the main program could continue with whatever its primary task was. See **data-directed control <51>**.

Contributor: AIWORD.DOC file (online: ARPA-net).

Reference

Nilsson, N.J. *Principles of Artificial Intelligence*, Tioga Pub. Co., Palo Alto, California, 1980.

58 Dempster-Shafer Theory

Alias: **Belief functions.**

This is a theory of evidence potentially suitable for knowledge-based systems, especially when domain knowledge can be articulated in categorical terms and the impact of each item of evidence is described as an assignment of probabilities to a select set of propositions. Such systems include strict taxonomic hierarchies, terminological definitions and descriptions of deterministic systems (*e.g.* electronic circuits). The probability $m(A)$ that is attached to a formula A represents the degree to which the evidence supports A, but $m(A)$ need not be equal to $1 - m(-A)$, since an item of evidence can lend support to a hypothesis while having no direct bearing on its negation. These "basic probabilities" can be visualised as probability masses that are constrained to stay within the subset (of worlds) with which they are associated, but are free to move over every point in the subset. From these basic probabilities we can derive upper and lower probabilities (Dempster) or belief functions and plausibilities (Shafer). The belief measure $Bel(A)$ stands for the probability that A logically follows from the evidence, given that all items of evidence are non-contradictory. This notion of "belief" often behaves differently than $P(A)$, the probability that A is true. The means of combining basic probabilities is using Dempster's Rule which is valid given independent items of evidence.

Contributor: Judea Pearl.

References

Shafer, G. *A mathematical theory of evidence.* Princeton University Press, Princeton, 1976.

Pearl, J. *Probabilistic Reasoning in Intelligent Systems: networks of plausible inference.* Morgan Kaufmann, San Mateo, California, 1988.

59 Dependency Directed Backtracking

Alias: **selective backtracking.**

An alternative to **chronological backtracking** where the backtrack point (the choice point that control is passed back to on failure) is determined by the nature of the failure. That is, the choice that caused the failure is undone whereas in chronological backtracking it is simply the last choice that is reconsidered. Some of the work done since the faulty choice may be independent of that choice, and with appropriate techniques much of this work can be retained.

Contributor: Lincoln Wallen.

References

Stallman, R.M. and Sussman, G.J. Forward reasoning and dependency-directed backtracking in a system for computer-aided circuit analysis. *Artificial Intelligence*, 9:135–196, 1977.

Pereira, L.M. and Porto, A. Selective backtracking. In K.L. Clark and S.A. Tärnlund, editors, *Logic programming*, Academic Press, London, 1982. APIC Studies in Data Processing, 16:107–117.

60 Depth-first Parsing

Amounts to a **depth-first search** <61> of the tree of alternatives which arise in the parsing process. Clearest in the context of **top-down** <243> parsing of a **context-free grammar** <45>. Suppose our grammar includes the following rules:

$$X \rightarrow Q\ R\ S$$
$$X \rightarrow U\ V\ W$$

Now suppose in the course of analysing a string, we are trying to find an X, which leads us to look for a Q, which we find. A choice then confronts us - do we look now for an R following the Q, or do we rather look for a U at the same place we found the Q? Given the possibility of ambiguity, either or both course may succeed. The first choice, which leads to a **backtracking parser**, is depth-first. The second choice, which leads to a **pseudo-parallel parser**, is **breadth-first** <26>. If the candidate string was in fact ambiguous, in the depth-first case we would find Q R S X_1 U V W X_2 in that order, whereas in the breadth-first case we would find Q U R V S W X_1 X_2.

Contributor: Henry Thompson.

Reference

Winograd, T. *Language as a cognitive process.* Addison-Wesley, Reading, Mass. and London, 1983.

61 Depth-first Search

Alias: **chronological backtracking.**

An uninformed **graph searching** strategy which searches the graph by exploring each possible path through it until either the required solution or a previously encountered node is encountered. The nodes are expanded in order of depth: with the deepest node expanded first and nodes of equal depth expanded in an arbitrary order. To prevent searching of an infinite path, a depth-bound is usually fixed and nodes below this depth are never generated, thus the strategy is neither guaranteed to produce the shortest path to the solution if one exists, nor to find a solution even if one exists.

Contributor: Dave Plummer.

Reference

Nilsson, N.J. *Principles of Artificial Intelligence.* Tioga Pub. Co., Palo Alto, California, 1980.

62 Deterministic Parsing

Non-determinism arises in a parsing process which proceeds on a word by word or constituent by constituent basis because of (often local) ambiguity in the grammar and lexicon. The degree of non-determinism can therefore be reduced by expanding the focus of attention to include more than just the 'next' constituent or word. Marcus has recently generated considerable interest with the claim that a small expansion of this sort allows English to be parsed deterministically in all but a few cases and in those it is claimed that people have difficulty as well.

Marcus and others pursuing this approach employ a **stack and buffer parsing** technique, in which words (and sometimes completed constituents) are accessed through a fixed length (typically 3 or 5 items) buffer, and partially completed constituents are held in a stack. Grammar rules are represented by **condition-action pairs**, where the conditions refer to the buffer and the stack, and the actions effect changes therein. Rules are grouped together for the purpose of activation and deactivation - only some groups of rules are active at any given time.

Strict determinism is ensured by the finiteness of the buffer and by requiring that all structures constructed at any point in the analysis must figure in the final result. It is an open question 'how much' of English, or other natural languages, can be analysed with grammars which can be parsed in this fashion.

Contributor: Henry Thompson.

Reference

Marcus, M. *A theory of syntactic recognition for natural language.* MIT Press, Cambridge, Mass., 1980.

63 Difference of Gaussians

This function is composed of the difference of two gaussian distributions and approximates $\nabla^2 G$ (the **laplacian <122>** of a gaussian), the operator which Marr and Hildreth proposed to be optimal for **edge detection <71>** in images. It also describes the 'mexican hat' weighting function of the receptive fields of retinal ganglion and LGN cells.

Contributors: T P Pridmore, S R Pollard, S T Stenton.

Reference

Marr, D. and Hildreth, E. Theory of edge detection. *Proc. Roy. Soc. Lond.*, B207:187–217, 1980.

64 Discrimination Learning

If a production system contains overly general rules, they will lead to **errors of commission** (i.e. the rule will fire when it should not). The discrimination learning method responds to such errors by comparing the **rejection context** (the situation in which the mistake was made) to a **selection context** (the last situation in which the rule applied correctly). Based on the differences it finds between the two contexts, the method creates one or more variants of the overly general rule that contain additional conditions or otherwise restrict its generality. The new rules may still be overly general, in which case the technique is applied recursively until variants are found that match only in the desired contexts. The discrimination method can learn **disjunctive concepts**, and when combined with a strengthening process to direct search through the rule space, it can deal with noise and learn heuristically useful rules despite incomplete representations.

Contributor: Pat Langley.

References

Anderson, J.R. and Kline, P.J. A learning theory and its psychological implications. In *Proceedings of IJCAI-79*, pages 16–21. International Joint Conference on Artificial Intelligence, 1979.

Langley, P. Language acquisition through error recovery. *Cognition and Brain Theory*, 1982.

65 Discrimination Net

Alias: **Discrimination Tree.**

A mechanism for allocating an input data item to its class by applying successive tests for different individual predicates; the terminal nodes of the net represent the results to be returned for the various possible sequences of predicates. A discrimination net (**D-net**) is thus a nest of IF...THEN...ELSE tests all applicable to one data item, or more formally, a binary, directed, **acyclic graph** with unary predicates at non-terminal nodes. An example of the use of a discrimination net of this basic kind is in **natural language generation** in choosing an output word for an input meaning representation. The basic mechanism can be extended by, for instance, using n-ary rather than binary graphs, with the corresponding replacement of simple feature tests by more complex branch selection functions, by the use of variables in the data item descriptions and net patterns, and by the use of sophisticated means of indexing. With such extensions, a net can be used, for example, to implement a **PLANNER**-style database optimised for retrieving individual assertions.

Discrimination nets have an obvious attraction when the set of classes involved is high; but clearly a prerequisite for their effective application is being able to identify clear test sequences for data items.

Contributor: Karen Sparck Jones.

Reference

Charniak, E., Riesbeck, C.K. and McDermott, D.V. *Artificial Intelligence Programming.* Lawrence Erlbaum Associates, Hillsdale, New Jersey, 1980.

66 Distance Transform

A class of transformations on binary images which assign to each pixel of an object its distance from the nearest object boundary. The actual transformation varies with the distance measure. Simple city block type measures can be implemented using shrink operations. Euclidean distance measures are harder to implement in parallel. The transformation is also used on lines, where the measure is some digital arc length.

The importance of such transforms arises from the assertion that any binary object can be reconstructed from the maxima of its distance function.

Contributor: Dave Reynolds.

67 Distributed Planning

When a problem can be divided into independent subproblems (cf **problem reduction <233>**), concurrent solution of them is possible and may be advantageous. For example, Kornfeld's **ETHER** language permits experimentation with concurrency in **heuristic search <98>**, and Smith has implemented a **contract-net** system motivated by the metaphor of manager - contractor linkage. The task of generating a plan may similarly be distributed over several concurrent planners, provided that each knows enough about the activities of the others to ensure consistency.

Contributor: Jim Doran.

References

Kornfeld, W.A. ETHER - a parallel problem solving system. In *Proceedings of IJCAI-79*, pages 490–492. International Joint Conference on Artificial Intelligence, 1979.

Davis, R. and Smith, R.G. Negotiation as a metaphor for distributed problem solving. *Artificial Intelligence*, 20:63–109, 1983.

68 Dynamic Programming

Dynamic programming is a **template matching <239>** technique which allows the template to be 'stretched' in a non-linear fashion to find a best fit with the input pattern. It is a general purpose technique with many applications. In speech research, it has been used for recognition of words from a limited vocabulary within spoken utterances (cf **dynamic time warping <69>**).

Contributor: Steve Isard.

69 Dynamic Time Warping

Alias: **dynamic programming in speech recognition.**

Two programs are provided, one that generates **linear predictive coding <128>** and autocorrelation coefficients from the speech utterances and the other that, using **dynamic programming <68>**, compares the test utterance with the reference utterances and finds the best match. The method used is Constrained Endpoint with 2-to-1 range of slope.

Contributor: Andrej Ljolje.

Reference

Rabiner, L.R., Rosenberg, A.E., and Levinso, S.E. Considerations in dynamic time warping algorithms for discrete word recognition. *IEEE Trans. ASSP*, 26(6):575, 1978.

70 Earley's Algorithm

The first published algorithm to bring the worst case asymptotic time complexity of **recognition** for unrestricted **context-free grammars <45>** down to cubic order in the number of words in the string to be parsed. Makes use of a **well-formed substring table**. See **caching <27>**.

Contributor: Henry Thompson.

Reference

Earley, J. An efficient context-free parsing algorithm.

71 Edge Detection

The purpose of edge detection is to locate places in images which correspond to informative scene events, such as a shadow or the obscuring boundary of an object. The projection of such events often produces steep gradients and discontinuities in image intensity, so the basic methods of edge detection are:

- differentiate the image and threshold the resulting gradient image
- differentiate the image twice and find the **zero-crossings** in the second derivative
- **template matching** <239>

Computationally, this normally involves **convolution** <49> of a neighbourhood operator with the image at every point in the image. Very many operators have been implemented, but because of the difficulty of precisely specifying the goal of edge detection, it is difficult to compare operator performance. The latest theories of edge detection involve applying operators to the same image at different resolutions in **resolution cones** in an attempt to provide a better description of the intensity changes present in the image.

Contributor: Bob Beattie.

Reference

Marr, D. and Hildreth, E. Theory of edge detection. *Proc. R. Soc. Lond.*, B207:187–217, 1980.

72 Epsilon Semantics

Alias: **probabilistic entailment, preferential entailment**

A **non-monotonic inference** system <155> in which defaults are interpreted as statements of high conditional probabilities, infinitesimally close to zero or one. The valid consequences are those statements that would acquire arbitrarily high probabilities whenever the probabilities assigned to the premises are made sufficiently high. Syntactical derivations require the solution of a series of propositional satisfiability problems. The system is suitable for maintaining consistency and enforcing specificity ordering, but does not support chaining and contraposition.

Contributor: Judea Pearl.

References

Pearl, J. *Probabilistic Reasoning in Intelligent Systems: networks of plausible inference*, Morgan Kaufmann, San Mateo, California, 1988 (Chapter 10).

Pearl, J. Probabilistic Semantics for Nonmonotonic Reasoning: A survey. In *Proceedings of First Intl. Conf. on Principles of Knowledge Representation and Reasoning* (KR'89), pages 505–516, 1989.

73 Expert System Shell

A shell is a domain-independent Expert Systems 'framework', i.e an inference engine with explanation facilities etc. but without any domain-specific knowledge. Provided the framework is a suitable one for a given problem, it may be possible by adding domain-specific knowledge to build a new Expert System with much less effort than beginning from scratch.

On the negative side, the use of a shell imposes a number of design decisions on e.g. the form in which knowledge is represented (for example, only **production rules** <**184**>), the means by which reasoning with uncertain knowledge is handled (eg **Bayesian Inference** <**15**>, **Dempster-Shafer Theory** <**58**>, etc.). These can considerably reduce the range of applicability of a particular shell.

Commercial shells are generally readily available for standard business computers (such as IBM PCs) but typically little or no attempt is made by suppliers to identify the range of applicability - and inapplicability - of their products.

Shells developed for research purposes (e.g. EMYCIN based on MYCIN, and KAS based on Prospector) generally offer more sophisticated facilities, but are frequently difficult to obtain outside the academic research community, are often poorly documented and even when available may be difficult to transfer to new systems.

Contributor: Max Bramer

Reference

Hayes-Roth, F., Waterman, D.A. and Lenat, D.B. (editors). *Building Expert Systems*, Volume 1. Addison-Wesley, Reading, Mass. and London, 1983.

74 Explanation-Based Learning

Explanation-Based Learning (**EBL**) techniques are knowledge-based and require a great deal of knowledge about the domain of the concept to be learned. Instead of providing several instances of a concept (as in **focussing <78>**), only a single example is required for a new concept to be learned. The idea is that a strong domain theory not only helps in describing or *explaining* the new concept, but also guides the generalisation process, such that a great deal can be learned from a single example.

Various EBL techniques have been developed: **Constraint Back Propagation**, **Explanation-Based Generalisation**, **Precondition Analysis <177>**; mostly in domains where there is a strong body of domain knowledge.

Contributor: Roberto Desimone.

References

DeJong, G. and Mooney, R. Explanation-based learning: an alternative view. *Machine Learning*, 1(2):145–176, 1986.

Mitchell, T.M., Keller, R.M. and Kedar-Cabelli, S.T. Explanation-based generalisation: a unifying view. *Machine Learing*, 1(1):47–80, 1986.

75 Extended Gaussian Image

A method of object shape representation in which an object is represented as a function on the unit sphere, by mapping points on the object surface to the point on the unit sphere with corresponding normal direction. The value of the function on the unit sphere is the sum (integral for a planar surface) of the absolute values of the inverse of the Gaussian curvatures of the corresponding surface points. The integral of the function over the unit sphere is the object's surface area. The representation rotates in correspondence with the object and for convex objects is unique (disregarding translation).

Contributor: R.M. Cameron-Jones

Reference

Horn, B.K.P. *Robot Vision.* MIT Press, Cambridge, Mass., 1986 (Chapter 16).

76 Fast Pattern Recognition Techniques

A technique for classifying very large bit vectors either by means of special purpose hardware or software has been developed. The system operates in two phases, a 'learning' phase and a 'use' phase. During the 'learning' phase examples of bit vectors together with a classifications are presented while during the 'use' phase unknown vectors are presented to the system and classified. The technique used is based on the Bledsoe and Browning n-tuple methodology.

Contributor: Igor Aleksander.

Reference

Aleksander, I. and Stonham, T.J. A guide to pattern recognition using random-access memories. *IEEE Journal of Computers & Digital Techniques*, 2(1), 1979.

77 Finding Common Paths

In a **production rule system** <184>, one method of **generalisation** involves replacing constant terms with variables. However, this can lead to unbound variables in the action side, and it is desirable to include additional conditions in the generalised rule which will instantiate these variables. Suppose the generalisation resulted from two rules with identical forms but differing constant terms. If one also has a long-term declarative memory available, then one can search through this memory for relations between differing symbols in the action sides of the specific rules and differing symbols in their condition sides. If analogous paths through the memory can be found for the two rules, a generalised path is created (again by replacing differing constants with variables) and this path is added as a set of conditions to the generalised rule. These conditions guarantee that all variables mentioned in the action side will be bound in the condition side. This method can be used to learn rules for solving algebra problems, for finding mappings between simple sentences and their meanings, and for discovering simple mathematical relations.

Contributor: Pat Langley.

Reference

Langley, P. Finding common paths as a learning mechanism. In *Proc. of the Third Nat. Conf.*, The Canadian Soc. for Computational Studies of Intelligence, 1980.

78 Focussing

Alias: **version space**.

A technique utilised by **concept learning** programs to record knowledge about the concept that is being learnt and to facilitate the updating of this knowledge as more information becomes available to the program. For this method the description space must consist of a number of attributes that a given example might have. These are conceptually represented either as sets of descriptions or as **lattices**, each branch of which represents a possible value for the attribute. Using the later representation, the technique records information by placing marks in these lattices to indicate which possible attribute values are not included in the concept being learnt. Upper marks indicate that all parts of the tree above the mark are definitely outside the concept (ie this is the maximally general description) and a lower mark indicates that all parts of the tree below the mark are definitely inside the concept (ie this is the maximally specific description). Between these marks there could be a grey region which is the area that the program is uncertain about. As the program gains more information the marks are moved to update the knowledge; positive instances of a concept are used to make the maximally specific description more general by moving the lower marker up, whilst negative instances are used to make the maximally general description more specific by moving the upper mark down. Once the upper and lower marks on all of the description trees coincide, the concept is completely specified and the program can report completion. The program can also detect failure if the marks become crossed (ie a lower mark above an upper one). This technique can handle most conjunctive concepts well but encounters difficulty handling disjunction, these difficulties may be surmountable by using multiple copies of the description space.

Contributor: Dave Plummer and Maarten van Someren.

References

Young, R.M., Plotkin, G.D. and Linz, R.F. Analysis of an extended concept-learning task. In *Proceedings of IJCAI-77*, page 285, International Joint Conference on Artificial Intelligence, 1977.

Mitchell. Generalisation as search. *Artificial Intelligence*, 18:203–226, 1982.

Bundy, A. and Silver, B. A critical survey of rule learning programs. In *Proceedings of ECAI-82*, pages 150–157, European Conference on Artificial Intelligence, 1982.

79 Formant

A speech signal can be described through formants; these are the principal resonances of the vocal tract, that determine which overtones of the fundamental larynx frequency will be allowed to pass through into the speech signal, and which will be damped. Each position of the articulators - the lips, tongue, jaw, etc. - gives rise to a characteristic pattern of formants. A speech signal can therefore be represented in terms of formant patterns which change over time, both for purposes of recognition and **synthesis-by-rule**.

Contributor: Steve Isard.

Reference

Gray, A.H. *Linear Prediction of Speech.* Springer-Verlag, New York, 1976.

80 Formant Synthesis

Basic sounds of a language can be characterised by their **formant <79>** frequencies. The formant pattern for a synthetic utterance can be created by interpolating between the formant values of the sounds composing the desired utterance. A speech wave can be computed from such a formant pattern, to be played through a digital-to-analogue converter, or the formant pattern can be used directly to excite a set of resonators, acting as an electrical analogue of the vocal tract.

Contributor: Steve Isard.

Reference

Klatt, D.H. Software for a cascade/parallel formant synthesizer. *Journal of Acoustic Society of America*, 67:971–995, 1980.

81 FORTRAN

FORTRAN is the programming Language considered by many to be the natural successor to **Lisp <129>** and **Prolog <187>** for A.I. research. Its advantages include:

1 it is very efficient for numerical computation (many A.I. programs rely heavily on number-crunching techniques).

2 A.I. problems tend to be very poorly structured, meaning that control needs to move frequently from one part of a program to another. FORTRAN provides a special mechanism for achieving this, the so-called **GOTO** statement.

3 FORTRAN provides a very efficient data structure, the **array**, which is particularly useful if, for example, one wishes to process a collection of English sentences each of which has the same length.

Contributor: Aloysius Hacker.

Reference

Coan, J.S. *Basic FORTRAN.* Hayden Book Co, Indianapolis, 1980.

82 Forward Search

Alias: **data-driven** search, **bottom-up** search, **forward chaining.**

A **state space** <226> can be searched from the initial state to the goal state, applying **operators** <159> forward (forward search); alternatively the state space can be searched from the goal to the initial state (**backwards search** <13>).

Contributor: Maarten van Someren.

Reference

Barr, A. and Feigenbaum, E.A. (editors). *The Handbook of Artificial Intelligence*, Volume 1. W. Kaufmann, Los Altos, California, 1981.

83 Fourier Transform

A method that transforms a (spatial or temporal) signal into the **frequency domain** by exploiting the fact that a signal can be represented as the sum (or integral) of a (usually infinite) series of weighted sinusoidal functions.

The fourier transform is useful for analysing and understanding the influence of linear operations on temporal or spatial signals. A good qualitative understanding about how a certain operation influences the signal in the frequency domain often helps to estimate limitations or possibilities that are otherwise not so easily recognised. This is most important for low-level vision applications. Fourier transforms are the most important tool for **Linear Systems Theory**.

The fourier transform is quite tedious computationally: i.e. the computational complexity of most one dimensional transforms is $O(Nlog(N))$ and two dimensional transforms is $O(N^2 log(N))$ where typically $N > 250$. Hence, it is usually impractical to implement the transform in software, although multiprocessor systems are now being used. Alternatives include use of special-purpose hardware or optical techniques.

Contributor: Fritz Seytter

References

Bracewell, R.N. *The Fourier transform and its applications.* McGraw-Hill, New York and London, 1986

Gaskill, J.D. *Linear systems, Fourier transforms, and optics.* Wiley, New York and Chichester, 1978

84 Frame

Alias: **script, schema.**

A principle for the large-scale organisation of knowledge introduced by Minsky, originally in connection with vision, but more generally applicable. A simple example is the **GUS** air trip frame, a structure with slots for the various elements of a trip e.g. passenger, source, destination, date, etc. which are instantiated in any particular application of the frame. Frames may be arbitrarily complex, and have procedures attached to the slots. Default values for the slots are helpful when frames are exploited in the absence of full instantiation data. The character of frames suggests a hierarchical organisation of sets of frames, but non-hierarchical filling of one frame slot by another is possible. Frame structures are often not deemed to imply temporal or causal relations between their slots, and are thus contrasted with **scripts** <209> but community usage in this respect is very inconsistent: one person's frame is another person's script, and vice versa. The main problem with systems with multiple frames is frame selection and replacement.

Contributor: Karen Sparck Jones.

Reference

Minsky, M. A framework for representing knowledge. In P.H. Winston, editor, *The Psychology of Computer Vision*, pages 211-277. McGraw-Hill, New York, 1975.

85 Functional Data Model

An **entity-relationship data model** with relationships expressed as functions which map their arguments to a single entity value or to a set of entities. Derived functions allow the definition of arbitrary new relationships in terms of existing ones. Different user views of data can be presented by defining appropriate derived functions. Updating of derived relationships is supported through procedures explicitly provided by the user.

Data manipulation languages, such as **DAPLEX**, have been added to the Functional Data Model to provide the notion of looping through entity sets to perform operations.

The Functional data model incorporates many of the ideas in earlier **semantic net <213>** systems, the **if-needed** and **if-added** theorems of the **PLANNER** and **CONNIVER** languages, and a range of data models.

Contributor: Austin Tate.

Reference

Shipman, D.W. The functional data model and the data language daplex. *ACM Transactions and Database Systems*, 6(1):140–173, 1981.

86 Functional Grammar

Functional grammar is a declarative expression of the relation between **surface structure** and **functional structure** in a natural language which is equally suitable for use in **parsing** and **generation**. The functional structure is a **directed acyclic graph** of attributes and values indicating the functional roles played by sentence constituents, e.g. subject, modifier ... Functional grammar has been adopted by a number of language generation systems as their grammatical basis.

Contributor: Henry Thompson.

References

Kay, M. Functional grammar. In *Proceedings of the Fifth Annual Meeting of the Berkeley Linguistic Society*, Berkeley Linguistic Society, 1979.

Appelt, D.E. TELEGRAM: a grammar formalism for language planning. In *Proceedings of the 21st Annual Meeting of the Association for Computational Linguistics*, Association for Computational Linguistics, 1983.

87 Functional Programming Language

Alias: **Applicative Language, Purely Functional Language**

A language where the value of an expression (its meaning) is determined solely by the values of its constituent parts. Such languages have no assignment statements, and make use of higher-order functions to avoid the need for imperative control constructs. Functional programs are often easier to reason about than their imperative counterparts, and subexpressions may be evaluated in any order, including in parallel, a property which can be exploited by concurrent architectures.

Contributor: Kevin Mitchell.

Reference

Henderson, P. *Functional Programming – Application and Implementation.* Prentice Hall, Englewood Cliffs, New Jersey, 1980.

88 Fuzzy Set Theory

Alias: **fuzzy logic**.

An extension of conventional set theory, with the grade of membership for an element in a set taking a value anywhere in the range [0,1], instead of 0 or 1 only. Developed as a means of avoiding the complexity in descriptions of subjective or ill-understood processes. Fuzzy logic extends the simple Boolean operators and can express implication.

Contributor: Janet Efstathiou.

References

Zadeh, L.A. Outline of a new approach to the analysis of complex systems and decision processes. *IEEE Trans. of Systems, Man and Cybernetics*, SMA-3:28–44, 1973.

Mamdani, E.H. and Gaines, B.R. *Fuzzy Reasoning and its Applications.* Academic Press, London, 1981.

89 Game Theoretic Semantics

The game-theoretic interpretation of logic is due to **Hintikka**. In this approach, any attempt to establish the truth or falsity of an expression, S, in an interpreted language, L, is correlated with a two-person, zero-sum, perfect information game, G(S), played according to the rules of L. These games can be thought of as constituting 'idealised processes of verification'. Informally, one can think of the two players as oneself and 'Nature', and the game consists of one seeking support for S, while Nature looks for a refutation.

Contributor: Patric Chan

Reference

Hintikka, J. *Logic, language games and information: Kantian themes in the philosophy of logic.* Clarendon Press, Oxford, 1973.

90 Generalised Cylinders

A currently popular method for three-dimensional **shape description**. Generalised cylinders are a class of objects obtained by extending the definition of a cylinder. An ordinary cylinder is the volume swept out by a circular disc moving perpendicular to a straight line segment that passes through its centre called the axis or spine of the cylinder. A generalised cylinder is then obtained by extending the definition to include things like:

1. A curved spine.
2. The radius of the disc varying as a function of the position along the spine.
3. The cross section being some planar figure other than a circle.
4. The cross section held at a non-perpendicular angle to the spine.

Contributor: Luis Jenkins.

References

Cohen, P.R. and Feigenbaum, E.A. (editors). *The Handbook of Artificial Intelligence*, Volume 3. Pitman, London, 1982.

Marr, D. Analysis of occluding contour. *Proc. Roy. Soc. London*, B197:441–475, 1977.

91 Generalised Phrase Structure Grammar

Alias: **GPSG**.

GPSG was a move away from the more traditional computational syntactic framework of transformation grammar. The main theoretical point of this formalism is that it is equivalent to **context-free grammars** <**45**>. The formalism differs from convention **phrase structure grammars** (**PSG**) in that it:

- Describes syntactic categories in terms of lists of feature and value pairs e.g. `[N +, V -, AGR [PER 3, PLU -]]` to represent a third person singular noun.
- Instead of conventional mother and daughters type rule, two equivalent notations are used, Immediate Dominance (ID) specifying which categories can dominate which daughters, *and* Linear Precedence (LP) rules specifying the order of these daughters.
- Feature passing conventions, specify default "copying" of features up and down the parse tree.
- Meta-rules can be used to define new ID/LP rules from other existing ones thus the meta-rules, and basic ID/LP rules effectively specify, if compiled out, a set of context free grammar rules.

Following GPSG a number of other similar syntactic theories were born under the global title of "**Unification Grammars**" <**249**> *e.g.* **Lexical Functional Grammar** (LFG), **Head Phrase Structure Grammar** (HPSG) and **Categorial Unification Grammar** (CUG).

Contributor: Alan W Black.

Reference

Gazdar, G., Klein, E., Pullum, F. and Sag, I. *Generalised Phrase Structure Grammar.* Blackwell, Oxford, 1985

92 Generate and Test

Alias: **model directed search.**

Problem solving can be viewed as the process of generating solutions from observed or given data. Unfortunately, it is not always possible to use direct methods (i.e. to go from data to solution directly), instead, we often have to use indirect or model-based methods. If we have a model of the real world, we can test the results we would expect from hypothetical solutions against those that we desire or observe in the real world.

The generate and test search technique is to generate some plausible solutions from some initial conditions and test them using the model. If necessary, we return to the generate stage, forming more solutions in the light of our test results then test these. This is repeated until an acceptable solution is found.

Examples of systems using generate and test search are **Meta-Dendral** and **Casnet.**

Contributor: Robert Corlett.

References

Feigenbaum, E.A., Buchanan, B.G. and Lederberg, J. On generality and problem solving: a case study using the Dendral program. In B. Meltzer and D. Michie, editors, *Machine Intelligence 6*, pages 165–196. Edinburgh University Press, Edinburgh, 1971.

Weiss, S.M., Kulikowski, C.A., Amarel, S. and Safir, A. A model based method for computer-aided medical decision making. *Artificial Intelligence*, 11:145–172, 1978.

93 Goal Structure

Alias: **holding periods, plan kernels, plan rationale, teleology**

Information about a plan which represents the purpose of the various plan parts in terms of the goals or subgoals they are intended to achieve. This can be contrasted with the **Plan Structure** <175> which contains details which may obscure information important to the finding of causes for planning or execution failures.

The **STRIPS MACROPS** (**operator tables** <160>) used such information for plan execution. Goal Structure has been used in a linear planner (**INTERPLAN**) and a **non-linear planner** (**NONLIN**) to guide search. It can be viewed as a **Meta-planning** <138> technique.

Contributor: Austin Tate.

References

Fikes, R.E. *Knowledge Representation in Automatic Planning Systems.* Technical Note 119, SRI, Menlo Park, California.

Tate, A. *Using Goal Structure to direct search in a Problem Solver.* PhD thesis, MIRU, Edinburgh, 1975.

94 Golay Neighbourhoods

A set of local patterns, devised by Golay for transformations on hexagonally connected **binary images**. They fall into the general class of **morphological transforms** ('hit or miss'). Each pattern is a hexagon of 'true', 'false' and 'do not care' entries. When a pattern matches the neighbourhood of a pixel in the image that pixel can be marked (to detect special points like line ends), set true (to 'thicken' the image) or set false (to 'thin' or 'skeletonise' the image). See **local grey-level operations** <130>.

Generalisations of such operations are now used for processing images with square connectivity.

Contributor: Dave Reynolds.

Reference

Golay, M.J.E. Hexagonal parallel pattern transformations. *IEEE Transactions on Computers*, C-18(8), 1969.

95 Gradient Space

A two dimensional space used to represent surface orientation in terms of its vertical and horizontal components. Thus the plane surface $-Z = P.X + Q.Y + C$ is represented by the point (P, Q) in gradient space. The steepness of the surface is $\sqrt{P^2 + Q^2}$ and the direction of the slope is $\tan^{-1}(Q/P)$. Such a representation does not make explicit the spatial location or extent of surface planes. Convex and concave edges and curvatures will be represented by lines in the gradient space, in the case of planar surface discontinuity edges these will be perpendicular to the edge in the image space, with order along the line determined by the convexity/concavity.

Contributors: T P Pridmore, S R Pollard, S P Stenton.

Reference

Draper, S.W. The use of gradient space and dual space in line drawing interpretation. *Artificial Intelligence*, 17:461–508, 1981.

96 Graph Matching

Relational structures are often represented as graphs with nodes connected by labelled arcs. The problem of matching two such structures is known as graph matching and can be achieved in a number of ways. Firstly a one-to-one mapping can be achieved between the nodes and arcs of each of the two graphs. This is known as **graph isomorphism**. Alternatively a one-to-one mapping can be achieved between one graph and a *subgraph* of the other. This is known as **double subgraph isomorphism**. Sometimes a perfect mapping between graphs is not required, some arcs and nodes being considered unimportant and omitted from the matching process.

Contributor: H.W. Hughes

Reference

Harary, F. *Graph Theory.* Addison-Wesley, Reading, Mass., 1969.

97 Heterarchy

In a **pipelined <172>** or **hierarchical process organisation**, data passes through a sequence of analytical or interpretive modules each of which acts independently of the rest. In a **heterarchical system**, modules may invoke other modules in the series to help with e.g. disambiguation of data. Winograd's program **SHRDLU**, in which syntactic analysis could make use of semantic modules on knowledge about the world was the most famous example. Shirai and others designed heterarchic image understanding programs. Heterarchy fell into disrepute when the work of Horn, Barrow and Tenenbaum suggested that far more disambiguation can be done autonomously by low levels than was previously thought. The fashion will change again when it is realised that in poor viewing conditions more sophisticated process organisation is required.

Contributor: Aaron Sloman.

Reference

Clowes, M.B. Man the creative machine. In J. Benthall, editor, *The limits of human nature.* Allen Lane, London, 1973

98 Heuristic Search

Alias: **best first search.**

A technique for state space searching, with the **state space <226>** represented as a graph. It uses domain-specific knowledge expressed as a numerical **evaluation function** which assigns a number to each node of the graph. At each stage of the search, heuristic search develops the tip node with the best numeric score. Tip nodes may be stored on an **agenda** in order of numeric score. See **A* Algorithm <2>**, **Alpha/Beta Pruning <6>**, **B* Algorithm <12>**, **Branch-and-bound algorithms <24>**, and **Minimax <141>** for examples of heuristic search.

Contributor: Dave Plummer.

Reference

Nilsson, N.J. *Principles of Artificial Intelligence.* Tioga Pub. Co., San Mateo, California, 1980.

99 Hierarchical Models

At the highest level a hierarchical model consists of a number of complex parts positioned within some global coordinate reference frame. Descending the hierarchy, each part is decomposed into more simple parts each with its own local coordinate frame. At each level the coordinate frame transformation between part and subpart is specified. By allowing degrees of freedom in the transformation it is possible to represent flexible joints between parts. Finally, at the lowest level of the hierarchy, the parts are decomposed into primitives (the basic building blocks) usually either volumes or surfaces (*eg.* **Generalised Cylinders <90>**). An example of this would be the modelling of a human hand. At the highest level would be the complete model of the hand. This would decompose into the palm, fingers and thumb. A finger would decompose further into the primitives representing them.

Contributor: H.W. Hughes

Reference

Brooks, R.A. Symbolic reasoning among 3D models and 2D images. *Artificial Intelligence*, 17(1): 285-349, 1981.

100 Hierarchical Planning

Alias: **plan refinement, top-down plan elaboration.**

The technique by which a hierarchical plan structure is generated by successive generation, from top to bottom, of its component levels. One variant of the technique, [Sacerdoti 78] makes use of **criticalities** assigned to operator preconditions. More generally, domain specific **plan elaboration rules** are required

[Tate 77]. Top-down plan elaboration is closely related to automatic top-down programming techniques [Barstow 79].

Contributor: Jim Doran.

References

Sacerdoti, E.D. Planning in a hierarchy of abstraction spaces. *Artificial Intelligence*, 5:115–135, 1978.

Tate, A. Generating project networks. In *Proceedings of IJCAI-77*, pages 888–893, International Joint Conference on Artificial Intelligence, 1977.

Barstow, D.R. An experiment in knowledge-based automatic programming. *Artificial Intelligence*, 12:73–119, 1979.

101 Hierarchical Synthesis

A technique used in the computer-based recognition of structure or objects. In a hierarchical synthesis recognition system, primitive or simpler features are recognised first, and then joined together to recognise larger objects in a bottom-up manner. For example, one might recognise the handle and bowl of a coffee cup first, and then verify that these were in positions compatible with being part of the same cup. This form of matching is often used as part of a **model-based vision** system <**143**>.

Contributor: Robert B. Fisher

Reference

Fisher, R. B. *From Surfaces to Objects: Computer Vision and Three Dimensional Scene Analysis.* John Wiley and Sons, Chichester, 1989.

102 High-emphasis Filtering

A method for sharpening images. The differentiation of an image is grossly interpreted in the frequency domain as filtering that emphasizes higher frequency components. As any linear operator in the spatial domain can be converted into an equivalent **transfer function** in the frequency domain, a linear operator designed to emphasize abrupt changes in intensity can be implemented by a transfer function designed to emphasize areas of high frequency. See also **Fourier Transform <83>**.

Contributor: Luis Jenkins.

Reference

Cohen, P.R. and Feigenbaum, E.A. (editors). *The Handbook of Artificial Intelligence*, Volume 3, pages 206–215. Pitman, London, 1982.

103 Hill Climbing

Hill climbing is a search method for finding a maximum (or minimum) of an evaluation function. It considers the local neighbourhood of a node, evaluates it, and follows those with the largest (or smallest) costs. Unlike other search strategies that use evaluation functions (e.g. **A* <2>** or informed **depth-first search <61>**) hill climbing is an irrevocable scheme, namely it does not permit us to shift attention back to previously suspended alternatives, even though they may have offered a greater alternative then the alternative at hand. This property is at the heart of both its computational simplicity and its shortcomings; it requires very little memory since alternatives do not need to be retained for future consideration. However, it is not guaranteed to lead to a solution, since it can get stuck on a plateau, or local extrema, or even wander on infinite uncontrolled paths, unless the guiding evaluation function is very informative.

Contributor: Rina Dechter.

Reference

Pearl, J. *Heuristics: intelligent search strategies for computer problem solving*, pages 35–36. Addison-Wesley, Reading, Mass. and London, 1984.

104 Hook

A hook is a piece of code or data-structure in an implementation which is made available to simplify later augmentation of the system. A good example is an evaluation algorithm that leaves sufficient information on the run-time stack for a good debugging package to be possible.

Contributor: Bruce Anderson.

105 Hough Technique

The Hough technique is a method of detecting parametric image features, such as curves. A point on a curve undergoes a transform to form a path in **parameter space** that represents all possible curves that could pass through that point. The parameter space is represented by an array whose elements are incremented each time a path passes across them. By repeating the transform for each point, local peaks are formed in parameter space representing points lying on the same curve in image space. The height of the peak indicates the number of points on the curve. To detect straight lines, for a point at position (x, y) the transform $r = xcos\theta + ysin\theta$ is usually used to produce a sinusoidal curve in (r, θ) parameter space. This technique can be used on any curve that can be parameterised, though the amount of computation required increases rapidly with the number of parameters.

Contributor: H.W. Hughes

Reference

Hough, P.V.C. Method and Means for Recognising Complex Patterns. *U.S. Patent 3,069,654*, 1962.

106 Image Data Structures

A wide variety of data structures are used to represent images. At the low level, raw grey-level image or binary images are represented by arrays of **pixels** (with square, triangular or hexagonal connectivity). Object boundaries are described by **fourier descriptors** or strings (Freeman chain code, symbolic strings). The adjacency of object regions is described by graph structures such as the **region adjacency graph**. Finally hierarchical or **pyramidal <192>** data structures which describe an image at a series of different levels or resolutions have proved useful (eg. **quad trees <193>**).

Contributor: Dave Reynolds.

Reference

Tanimoto, S. and Klinger, A. *Structured Computer Vision.* Academic Press, New York, 1980.

107 Image Flow Estimation

The estimation of the two-dimensional velocity field which maps the image intensity pattern at one time instant on to that at the succeeding time instant. The image flow is equivalent to the **optical flow <162>** if the image intensity value for the (changing) image point corresponding to a point in the world remains constant. Methods for recovering image flow are usually based on the **motion constraint equation** (which relates the local image velocity to local spatial and temporal intensity derivatives) and thus are hindered by the **aperture problem** - the local irrecoverability of velocity along a direction of zero intensity gradient. Hence methods for flow recovery at points other than intensity extrema require the imposition of further constraints, and **regularisation <201>** methods are commonly used for flow estimation on curves or over regions.

Contributor: R.M. Cameron-Jones

Reference

Nagel, H.H. On the estimation of optical flow: relations between different approaches and some new results. *Artificial Intelligence*, 33:299–324, 1987

108 Image Segmentation

Segmentation attempts to identify important features in an image, such as lines or regions of a uniform colour. In **low-level segmentation**, pixels are grouped together using techniques like thresholding or (for edges) **convolution <49>**. In **high-level segmentation**, expectations from models are used to guide the use of such low-level feature detectors. See also **Model-Based Vision <143>**.

Contributor: Dave Reynolds.

References

Fu, K.S. and Mui, J.K. A survey on image segmentation. *Pattern Recognition*, 13:3–16, 1981.

Brady, M. Computational approaches to image understanding. *ACM Computer Surveys*, 14:3-71, 1982.

109 Incidence Calculus

Alias: **Probabilistic Logic.**

A multi-valued logic in which the value of a formula is a set of situations in which the formula is true. These situations can be possible worlds, models or members of any set of objects. The values of composite formula are defined to be set theoretic combinations of the values of their sub-formulae, *e.g.* the value of a conjunction is the intersection of the values of the conjuncts. The formulae can be assigned a number, *e.g.* a probability, by applying an arithmetic function to their assigned sets, *e.g.* the sum of the probabilities of each member of the set. In this way incidence calculus can be used to represent the uncertainty of a formulae, *e.g.* as a probability. The main advantage of this indirect route of assigning probabilities is that the correlation between two formulae is implicitly represented by the degree of intersection between formulae. Thus it is not necessary to assume conditional independence. When a new conclusion is deduced from some hypotheses the value of the conclusion is not completely determined by the values of the hypotheses, but it is possible to calculate tight upper and lower bounds on value of the conclusion.

Contributor: Alan Bundy.

Reference

Bundy, A. Incidence Calculus: A Mechanism for Probabilistic Reasoning. *Journal of Automated Reasoning*, 1:263–284, 1985. Also available as DAI Research Paper No 216, Edinburgh University.

110 Inferno

Inferno is a conservative approach to uncertainty. It is based on a probabilistic approach to uncertainty, but, unlike most similar schemes, does not make any assumptions about relationships between propositions (eg. independence). It is, however, possible to assert such relationships in Inferno if they exist. The method is essentially based on upper and lower probabilities (see **Dempster-Shafer Theory** <**58**>) which give upper and lower bounds on the probability of each proposition. Each time one of these bounds change, the bounds on related propositions are checked and suitably modified to satisfy a set of propagation constraints. These constraints are based on the inequality

$$max(P(A), P(B)) \leq P(A \text{ or } B) \leq P(A) + P(B).$$

One unique feature of Inferno is its ability to detect and suggest corrections for contradictions and inconsistencies in its data. If, the propagation constraints cannot provide valid values for the bounds, Inferno invokes a method similar to **dependency directed backtracking** <**59**> to suggest changes to the data that would remove the inconsistency.

Contributor: Robert Corlett.

Reference

Quinlan, J.R. Inferno: a cautious approach to uncertain inference. *The Computer Journal*, 26(3), 1983.

111 Interactions Between Sub-Solutions

Whenever a planner makes the assumption that conjunctive goals can be solved independently (either one after the other or in parallel) there is likely to be interference between the partial solutions. Techniques have been developed to recognise and correct for these interactions between solutions to conjunctive goals.

Sussman's **HACKER** solved problems by assuming an ordered solution was feasible. It then had **critics** to recognise interactions and HACKER was often able to repair the plan by re-arranging the steps in the plan. In his **INTERPLAN** program, Tate's approach was to abstract the original goals and to determine holding periods over which these could be assumed to be true. INTERPLAN analysed this '**goal structure**' with a view towards ordering the approach taken to solve the sub-goals to ease conflict situations. Waldinger developed an approach called '**goal regression**' in which a solution to one goal was built and then the plan was constructively modified to achieve the further plans (by moving new goals backwards through a partial plan to a position where they did not interfere). A scheme similar to that used by Waldinger was incorporated in WARPLAN , a planner written in **Prolog <187>**.

All the above mentioned planners produce their plans as a linear sequence of actions. **Non-linear planner <154>** NONLIN, also dealt with interactions between sub-goals in plans which are produced as partially ordered networks of actions.

Contributor: Austin Tate (adapted from Mark Stefik).

References

Sussman, G.J. *A computational model of skill acquisition.* American Elsevier, New York, 1975.

Tate, A. Interacting goals and their use. In *Proceedings of IJCAI-79*, International Joint Conference on Artificial Intelligence, 1979.

Waldinger, R. *Achieving several goals simultaneously.* Technical Note 107, SRI AI Center, Menlo Park, 1975.

Warren, D.H.D. *WARPLAN: A system for generating plans.* Memo 76, Dept. of Artificial Intelligence, Edinburgh, 1974.

112 Interval Calculus

Interval calculus stands for a description of temporal relationships in which time is treated in terms of intervals. There are 13 possible primitive relations between pairs of intervals, *e.g.* "X before Y", "X meets Y". The relationships between intervals are maintained in a network where the nodes represent individual intervals and the arcs label possible relations between the intervals. This allows one to construct non-primitive relations. There are rules of transitivity, allowing a computationally effective inference process, *e.g.* "if (X during Y) and (Y meets Z) then (X before Z)".

Contributor: Sundermeyer.

Reference

Allen, J. Toward a general model of action and time. *Artificial Intelligence*, 23, 1984.

113 Intrinsic Images

The term was first used by Barrow and Tenenbaum (1976) to refer to a registered 'stack' of retinotopic maps each of which makes explicit the value of a certain property 'intrinsic' to the surfaces in the scene. The intrinsic images all have the same viewer centred coordinate system but carry information about different surface properties, such as: surface orientation, depth, reflectance, colour, texture and **Optical Flow <162>** (this last intrinsic image describes the instantaneous velocity flow field in the scene). The computation of the intrinsic images is non-trivial, many of them are underdetermined when considered independently but global consistency constraints can be cooperatively exploited, eg surface boundary information carried by the reflectance image can be used to constrain the computation of the surface orientation from shading information.

Over the last five years there have been considerable advances in understanding of the problems of computing the different intrinsic images. Their particular importance is that they are a vital stage in the computation of a representation intermediate between the lowest levels of image processing, whose descriptions are essentially 2D pictorial or iconic descriptions of the scene, and the higher levels of processing which describe the shapes of objects in terms of an **object-centred <157>** viewer independent coordinate system. The intrinsic images are the first representation at which information concerning the 3D structure of the scene is made explicit. Object recognition schemes that have attempted to recover 3D shape descriptions directly from 2D shape descriptions have, to put it mildly, struggled. See also **$2\frac{1}{2}$-D Sketch <1>**.

Contributor: Jon Mayhew.

References

Brady, M. Computational approaches to image understanding. *Computer Surveys*, 14(1):2–71, 1982.

Barrow, H.G. and Tenenbaum, J.M. Computational vision. In *Proc IEEE 6*, pages 572–596, IEEE, 1981.

114 Invariant

An invariant is an assertion about a data structure or database which is expected to be true at certain times. For example a **resolution <204>** data base should not contain empty clauses between queries. An **invariant queue** is a queue which contains at least one entry for each violation of a given invariant. Processing an entry from an invariant queue should remove a violation of the invariant. If an invariant queue is empty then the invariant should hold. A given system can have many invariants and many invariant queues. An **invariant violation demon** can be used to cope with invariants; such a **demon <57>** triggers when an **invariant** is violated, either correcting the violation immediately or placing an entry on an invariant queue.

Contributor: D. McAllester.

Reference

McAllester, D. *Reasoning Utility Package User's Manual Version One*. Memo 667, MIT AI Lab, Cambridge, Mass., April 1982.

115 Inverse Resolution

This machine learning technique involves the construction of first-order logic clauses by inverting single **resolution** <**204**> steps. Two inverse resolution operators exist, the V and the W. The V operator takes the consequent clause and one of the antecedent clauses of a resolution step and constructs the other antecedent. The W operator takes two consequents of two resolutions which have a common antecedent and constructs all three antecedents, thus introducing a new predicate symbol. Inverse resolution is provably capable of constructing a wide class of theories, including **recursive** theories <**197**>, from ground unit examples.

Contributor: Stephen Muggleton.

Reference

Muggleton, S. and Buntine, W. Machine invention of first-order predicates by inverting resolution. In *Proceedings of the Fifth International Conference on Machine Learning*, pages 339–352. Morgan Kaufmann, San Mateo, California, 1988.

116 ISA Hierarchy

Alias: **inheritance hierarchy**, **type hierarchy**.

Strictly a straightforward manifestation of class membership, found useful in knowledge representation because property specifications for classes need only be explicitly indicated once, i.e. at the highest level, since they are automatically inherited by subclasses. ISA relationships are often found in a **semantic net** <**213**>. This form of ISA relationship must be clearly distinguished from

ISA relationships between individuals and the classes of which they are members. This second version of the ISA relationship is also found in semantic nets.

Contributor: Karen Sparck Jones.

Reference

Fahlman, S.E. *NETL, a system for representing and using real-world knowledge.* MIT Press, Cambridge, Mass., 1979.

117 Island Parsing

The adaptation of **augmented transition network** <10> parsing to deal with the problems presented by, for example, speech where the terminal symbols of the grammar cannot be certainly identified in correct linear sequence in the input. Bidirectional parsing is initiated from any plausibly identified node in the network, an island, providing hypotheses to assist the identification of uncertain input items. However parsing is complicated by the fact that tests and actions may be context dependent, and may not be executable because the required information for leftward input items is not yet available.

Contributor: Karen Sparck Jones.

Reference

Woods, W. et al. *Speech Understanding Systems, Final Report Vol.4.* Report 3438, Beranek and Newman Inc., 1976.

118 Iterative Deepening

An uninformed graph search algorithm which is a good compromise between the efficiency of **Depth-first Search** <61> and the admissibility of **Breadth-first Search** <26>. Iterative deepening performs a complete search of the search space (often using a depth-first search strategy) up to a maximum depth d. If no solutions can be found up to depth d, the maximum search depth is increased to $d+1$, and the search space is traversed again (starting from the top node). This strategy ensures that iterative deepening, like breadth-first search, always terminates in an optimal path from the start node to a goal node whenever such a path exists (this is called admissibility); but it also allows implementation as an efficient depth-first search. Iterative deepening is optimal in both time and space complexity among all uninformed admissible search strategies.

At first sight it might look as if iterative deepening is inefficient, since after increasing the cut-off depth from d to $d+1$, it redoes all the work up to level d in order to investigate nodes at level $d+1$. However, since typical search spaces grow exponentially with d (because of a constant branching factor), the cost of searching up to depth $d+1$ is entirely dominated by the search at the deepest level $d+1$: If b is the average branching rate of the search space, there are $b^{(b+1)}$ nodes at depth $d+1$, which is the same as the total number of nodes up to depth d. In fact, it can be shown that among all uninformed admissible search strategies, iterative deepening has the lowest asymptotic complexity in both time ($O(b^d)$) and space ($O(d)$). Breadth-first search on the other hand is only asymptotically optimal in time, and is very bad (exponential) in space. The actual time complexity of breadth-first search (as opposed to the asymptotic complexity) is of course lower than that for iterative deepening (namely by the small constant factor $b/b-1$), but this is easily offset by the difference in space-complexity in favour of iterative-deepening. Thus, iterative-deepening is asymptotically optimal in both time and space, whereas breadth-first is asymptotically optimal only in time and really bad in space, while the actual complexities of iterative-deepening and breadth-first are very close.

Iterative deepening can also be applied to informed search strategies, such as **A* <2>**. This modified version of A* is again optimal in both time and space among all informed admissible search strategies.

Contributor: Frank van Harmelen.

Reference

Korf, R. Depth-first iterative-deepening: an optimal admissible tree search. *Artificial Intelligence*, 27(1):97–109, 1985.

119 Junction Dictionary

Within the **blocks world** domain, only a restricted set of edge types of vertices, and thus line junctions in the image, exist. A junction dictionary can be constructed for line labellings of each member of this set. Of all the possible line labellings (which would imply a potentially large dictionary), only a small subset are in fact physically possible. See also **relaxation labelling <203>** and **line labelling <127>**.

Contributors: T P Pridmore, S R Pollard, S P Stenton.

Reference

Waltz, D. Understanding line drawings of scenes with shadows. In P.H. Winston, editor, *The Psychology of Computer Vision*, McGraw-Hill, New York, 1975.

120 Kinematics

Analysis of the kinematics of mechanisms can provide a technique for rational design of manipulators and workspaces. Mechanical arrangements for robot manipulators vary widely among operational robots, the most common configurations being best described in terms of their coordinate features: cartesian, spherical, and articulated. In a cartesian robot, a wrist is mounted on a rigid framework to permit linear movement along three orthogonal axes, rather like a gantry crane or (for two axes) a graph plotter; the resulting workspace is box-shaped. The cylindrical robot has a horizontal arm mounted on a vertical column which is fixed to a rotating base. The arm moves in and out; a carriage moves the arm up and down along the column, and these two components rotate as a single element on the base; the workspace is a portion of a cylinder. The spherical robot is similar to the turret of a tank: the arm moves in and out, pivots vertically, and rotates horizontally about the base; the workspace is a portion of a sphere. An articulated robot is more anthropomorphic: an upper arm and forearm move in a vertical plane above a rotating trunk. The limbs are connected by revolute joints; the workspace approximates a portion of a sphere. For all robots, additional degrees of freedom are provided at the extremity of the arm, at the wrist. Wrists generally allow rotation in two or three orthogonal planes. To make proper use of a robot arm, transformations between encoded axis values (joint angles, etc) and more convenient coordinate systems must be computed at high speed. Transforming a set of axis values to a position and orientation in space is called the forward kinematics transformation. The reverse transformation is used to convert a desired position and orientation in space into commanded axis values.

Contributor: W.F. Clocksin.

References

Engleberger, J.F. *Robotics in Practice.* IFS Publications, Kogan, London, 1980.

Simons, G.L. *Robots in Industry.* NCC Publications, 1980.

Paul, R.P. *Robot Manipulators: mathematics, programming and control.* MIT Press, Cambridge, Mass., 1981.

121 Lambda calculus

Various formal systems based on that invented by Church to formalise the properties of functions acting on arguments and being combined to form other functions. This involves "lambda-abstraction". The function f given by

$$f(x) = x + 1$$

can be written using lambda-abstraction as

$$f = \lambda x.x + 1$$

so that

$$f(1) = (\lambda x.x + 1)(1) = 2$$

Application is written as juxtaposition, *eg.* fx for $f(x)$. Terms made up using application and lambda abstraction can be manipulated in various ways, *eg.* rename bound variables (**alpha conversion**), and rewrite $(\lambda x.fx)a$ as fa (**beta reduction**).

This is the formalism that underlies **Lisp <129>**.

Contributor: Alan Smaill.

References

Hindley, J.R. and Seldin, J.P. *Introduction to combinators and the lambda-calculus.* Cambridge University Press, Cambridge, England, 1986.

Barendregt, H.P. *The lambda calculus, its syntax and semantics*, revised edition. North-Holland, Amsterdam and Oxford, 1984.

122 Laplacian

The Laplacian is the lowest (second) order circularly symmetric differential operator. When convolved with a 2-D function (e.g. an image) it computes the non-directional second derivative of that function. See also **convolution <49>**.

Contributors: T P Pridmore, S R Pollard, S T Stenton.

Reference

Marr, D. *Vision: a computational investigaion into the human representation and processing of visual information.* W.H. Freeman, New York, 1982.

123 Lazy Evaluation

Alias: **call-by-need**

A parameter passing mechanism in which the evaluation of an argument is postponed until its value is actually required. Used as an alternative to **call-by-value** where arguments to a function are evaluated before the function is called. The technique is particularly useful for the construction and manipulation of infinite data structures. See also **Delayed Evaluation <56>**.

Contributor: Kevin Mitchell.

Reference

Peyton Jones, S.L. *The Implementation of Functional Programming Languages.* Prentice Hall, Englewood Cliffs, London, 1987.

124 Learning from Solution Paths

Starting with only the legal conditions on a set of **operators <159>**, a strategy learning system can employ weak methods to search a problem space. Once a solution path has been found, it can be used to assign credit and blame to instances of these operators. If a move leads from a state on the solution path to another state on the solution path, it is labelled as a **positive instance** of the responsible operator. However, if a move leads from a state on the solution path to a state not on the path, it is marked as a **negative instance.** These classifications can then be input to a condition-finding mechanism (such as the generalisation, discrimination or **version space <78>** methods); which will determine the heuristically useful conditions under which each operator should be applied.

Contributor: Pat Langley.

Reference

Sleeman, D., Langley, P. and Mitchell, T.M. Learning from solution paths: an approach to the credit assignment problem. *AI Magazine*, 3(2):48–52, 1982.

125 Lexical Access

There are various techniques for accessing lexical information ranging from the sensible, e.g. the use of a tree structure on a letter-per-branch basis, to the ridiculous, e.g. linear search. The larger the lexicon the more important it becomes to relate word frequency to the access method. In English, for example, a mere 100 word types account for over 50% of the word tokens in running text. It also becomes more important to take a general approach to the problems of inflected forms, e.g. past tenses, plurals, and spelling rules or morphographemics **<146>**.

Contributor: Henry Thompson.

References

Kay, M. Morphological and syntactic analysis. In A. Zampolli, editor, *Linguistic Structures Processing*, pages 131-234 North Holland, Amsterdam and Oxford, 1977.

Kaplan, R.M. and Kay, M. *Word recognition*. Technical Report, Xerox Palo Alto Research Center, 1982.

126 Library-based Planning

Alias: **Variant Planning**

Instead of the plan required for a given task being constructed de novo, a plan library is maintained and, given a particular task, a relevant plan is found in the library and adapted to the current need. This may involve keeping with the plans in the library information about their derivation.

Contributor: Jim Doran

Reference

J. Carbonell. A computational model of analogical problem solving. In *Proceedings IJCAI-81*, pages 147–152. International Joint Conference on Artificial Intelligence, 1981.

127 Line Labelling

Huffmann and Clowes conceptualised the task of interpreting straight line drawings in terms of attaching labels like '**concave**', '**convex**', '**occluding**' to lines, interpreted as depicting object edges. See **junction dictionary** <**119**> and **relaxation labelling** <**203**>.

Contributor: Aaron Sloman.

Reference

Clowes, M.B. On seeing things. *Artificial Intelligence*, 2:79–116, 1971.

128 Linear Predictive Coding

If one approximates the vocal tract as a series of fixed length tubes (which is equivalent to representing it as an all-pole digital filter) it becomes possible to predict successive samples of the speech wave as linear combinations of previous samples. The coefficients in the linear combination characterize the shape of the vocal tract. A sequence of sets of coefficients can be used to characterize the changing shape of the vocal tract over time. This representation is widely used because of the particularly efficient algorithms associated with it.

Contributor: Steve Isard.

129 Lisp

Since its definition in 1958 by John McCarthy, Lisp (an acronym for **LIS**t **P**rocessing) has been the primary AI programming language. The reasons for its success are related not only to its early development but also to its technical characteristics:

- **Applicative style**: pure Lisp is a functional language whose underlying ideas are directly related to **Lambda calculus** <**121**>. Thus the increment function:

  $$\texttt{ADD1} = \lambda \texttt{n.n} + 1$$

  can be defined in Lisp as:

  ```
  (DEFUN ADD1(n)(+ n 1))
  ```

- **Program as data**: programs are represented in the same data structure as other data, namely the **list**. A program can be manipulated as any other data structure.

The first characteristic is true only of what is called *pure Lisp*. All the existing different dialects of Lisp also have control structures for imperative programming. Among the most important dialects are: MACLISP (from MIT) [Winston and Horn 81], FRANZ LISP (a dialect of MACLISP developed at Berkeley) [Wilensky 84] and INTERLISP (developed by BBN and Xerox). Lately a big effort has been made to unify all the different dialects in an unique language called COMMON LISP [Steele 84].

Contributor: Fausto Giunchiglia.

References

Winston, P.H. and Horn, B.K.P. *LISP.* First Edition, Addison-Wesley, Reading, Mass., 1981.

Wilensky, R. *LISPcraft.* W.W. Norton and Company, New York and London, 1984.

Steele, G.L. Jr. *Common Lisp.* Digital Press, Burlington, 1984.

Winston, P.H. and Horn, B.K.P. *LISP.* Second Edition, Addison-Wesley, Reading, Mass., 1984.

130 Local Grey-level Operations

Alias: **image morphology**.

A class of transformations on grey-level image which replace each **pixel** (in parallel) by some function of its neighbouring pixels.

In pointwise operations the new pixel value is independent of the neighbourhood, for example simple grey scale remapping such as histogram equalisation.

Linear operations (**convolution <49>**) are used for filtering (local averaging etc) and feature detection (such as **edge detection <71>**).

Non-linear operations can be developed using local minimum and local maximum functions to replace summation. Such operations can also be regarded as grey level generalisations of binary morphological operations using the **fuzzy logic <88>** based replacement of AND by MIN and OR by MAX. Illustrative operations are 'shrink' and 'expand' (also called 'erode' and 'dilate'). In a shrink operation a 'true' pixel is changed to 'false' if there is a 'false' pixel in some defined neighbourhood of it. Similarly for expand. For example, if the neighbourhoods are defined as 3x3 squares then shrink will delete all edge pixels.

Some of these types of transformations have been generalised to three dimensional binary images.

Contributor: Dave Reynolds.

Reference

Serra, J. *Image Analysis and Mathematical Morphology.* Academic Press, London, 1982.

131 Logic Programming

The core idea of logic programming is that it is possible to provide a procedural semantics for statements in certain (usually classical) logical formalisms. In theory, programming is then reduced to providing a program specification that is represented as a set of axioms. This is handed over to a sound and complete theorem prover. The theorem prover constructs a proof that there is a solution. If there is a solution then further useful information can usually be extracted from the proof. The main justification for such an approach is that classical logic is well understood and that, as a consequence, it is possible to provide systems which have a rigorous, theoretical foundation.

In order for such systems to be useful it is necessary that the formalism is sufficiently powerful and desirable that it is also sufficiently expressive. The best-known example of attempt to realise such a system is **Prolog <187>** which is based on a resolution theorem prover **<204>**. Programs are written in the Horn clause form **<36>** of first order **predicate logic <180>**.

There is an extensive literature on the properties of Prolog (and some of its variations) vis-a-vis soundness and completeness. Note that the ideal has not been attained in practice as a) the fixed control strategy built into most Prolog interpreters does not always find all solutions, b) some explicit control (procedural element) is usually required and c) programs often require side effects which undermine the declarative semantics. There are also some difficulties in connection with extending the expressiveness of Prolog, in particular, the problems of negation <**151**> and equality.

The term "logic programming" is often taken to be synonymous with "Prolog". This is not correct, however, as the field of logic programming also includes the so-called committed choice languages. These languages use a Prolog-like formalism but are designed for various forms of parallel execution. Examples include PARLOG, GHC and CP. Such languages lack a clear declarative semantics. Other systems have been built which explore various extensions, alternative control regimes or methods for automating proof search other than resolution.

Contributor: Paul Brna

References

Balbin, I. and Lecot, K. *Logic Programming: A Classified Bibliography.* Wildgrass Books, Fitzroy, Australia, 1985.

Hogger, C. *Introduction to Logic Programming.* Academic Press, London, 1984.

132 Logics of Knowledge and Belief

In order to construct a plan it is often necessary for an agent to take into account the fact that he or she may require certain pieces of knowledge to execute the plan, knowledge which may be obtainable by performing certain actions. An agent may also need to take into account the knowledge and beliefs of other agents. So in designing an intelligent agent we need to employ some method for reasoning about knowledge and belief. A logic of knowledge or belief can be obtained by adding to some system of logic some means of expressing such facts as "A knows that p" or "A believes that p" where "A" designates an agent and "p" a proposition. So we could introduce names of agents and variables ranging over agents together with operators such as K and B, so that "$K(A,p)$" means that A knows that p and "$B(A,p)$" means that A believes that p.

In Artificial Intelligence there are basically two approaches to the construction of a logic of knowledge or belief. There is a sentential approach where we associate with each agent a set of sentences which constitutes the agents base beliefs. We say that an agent believes a proposition just in case the agent can prove the proposition from these base beliefs. An agent knows a proposition if he or she believes the proposition and it is true. There is also an approach which construes the K operator as analogous to the L operator in **Modal Logic** **<142>**. Here we associate with each agent sets of possible worlds. We say that an agent believes a proposition in a given world just in case that proposition holds in every world accessible for an agent in a given world.

Contributor: Colin Phillips.

References

Moore, R.C. A formal theory of knowledge and action. In J.R. Hobbs and R.C. Moore, editors, *Formal theories of the commonsense world*, Ablex Pub. Corp., Norwood, 1985.

Konolige, K. A first order formulation of knowledge and action in a multi-agent planning system. In J.E. Hayes, D. Michie and Pao, editors, *Machine Intelligence 10*. Artificial Intelligence Center, SRI International, Menlo Park, 1980.

133 Macro Operators

Alias: **MACROPS**, **triangle table**.

It is possible to combine a sequence of **operators** <**159**> to build a new one, a macro operator, that has the effect of the sequence. Its list of preconditions contains all preconditions of the first operator of the sequence, plus those of later operators in so far as they have not been satisfied by previous operators in the sequence. The ADD and DELETE LISTS are determined in the same way.

Macro operators can be represented like 'basic' operators and be added to the set of existing operators. This is a form of **learning** that will reduce search in new problems.

Contributor: Maarten van Someren.

Reference

Fikes, R.E., Hart, P.E., and Nilsson, N.J. Learning and executing generalised robot plans. *Artificial Intelligence*, 3:251–288, 1972.

134 Marker-passing

Alias: NETL

This technique involves performing parallel searches through an **semantic net <213>** by the placing of simple binary tags, called marks, on memory nodes. An example of the use of marker-passing would to query a network as to the COLOR of an Elephant named CLYDE. The elements next to each of these would be marked, as would their neighbours in turn. The only node marked from each starting place would be GRAY, the correct answer. Much is now know about ther limitations of such a technique and the mathematics of inheritance hierarchies. See also **Symbolic Marker-passing <237>**

Contributor: James A.Hendler

Reference

Fahlman, S.E. *NETL: a system for representing and using real world knowledge.* MIT Press, Cambridge, Mass., 1979.

135 Markov Fields

A probabilistic description of a system of variables that interact locally, organised as vertices in a graph. A Markov field encodes the assumption that each variable is influenced by only its nearest neighbors. In image processing, Markov fields are used to represent the correlations between adjacent picture cells. In **neural nets**, Markov fields represent the energy associated with each state.

Contributor: Judea Pearl.

Reference

Geman, S. and Geman, D. Stochastic relaxation, Gibbs distributions and the bayesian restoration of images. *IEEE Trans on PAMI*, 6:721–742, 1984.

136 Maximum Cardinality Search

A method of ordering nodes in a graph which, whenever possible, guarantees the following condition: no two nodes will be linked to a successor node unless the two are linked together. The ordering consists of sequentially selecting a node that makes the largest number of connections with those selected earlier. This search yields close to optimal orderings for conducting **adaptive consistency**. It is also used in **constraint satisfaction** <**43**> and probabilistic reasoning problems to transform a network into a tree of clusters, thus facilitating local propagation and relaxation.

Contributor: Rina Dechter

References

Dechter, R. and Pearl, J. Tree clustering for constraint networks, *Artificial Intelligence*, 38:353–366, 1989.

Tarjan, R. E. and Yannakakis, M. Simple linear-time algorithms to test chordality of graphs, test acyclicity of hypergraphs and selectively reduce acyclic hypergraphs. *SIAM J. Computing*, 13:566-579, 1984.

137 Means/ends Analysis

A technique for controlling search. Given a current state and a goal state, an **operator** <**159**> is chosen which will reduce the difference between the two.

This operator is applied to the current state to produce a new state, and the process is recursively applied to this new state and the goal state.

Contributor: Alan Bundy.

Reference

Newell, A. and Simon, H.A. GPS, a program that simulates human thought. In E.A. Feigenbaum and J. Feldman, editors, *Computers and Thought*, pages 279–293. McGraw Hill, New York, 1963.

138 Meta-action Oriented Planning

Alias: **opportunistic planning, agenda based planning, meta-planning**

The operations that a planner performs upon the plans it is working with (e.g. expansion, reduction) are referred to as "**meta-actions**". A flexible and opportunity based choice of which meta-action to perform next can be achieved by maintaining a heuristic scheduler, where the tasks on the agenda correspond to possible meta-action executions. There is a close relationship to blackboard architectures <**20**>. Meta-planning occurs when a planner constructs plans which involve explicit representations of meta-actions. See also **meta-level inference <139>**.

Contributor: Jim Doran

References

Hayes-Roth, B. and Hayes-Roth, F. A cognitive model of planning. *Cognitive Science*, 3:275–310, 1979.

Stefik, M. Planning and meta-planning (Molgen: part 2). *Artificial Intelligence*, 16:141–170, 1981.

Currie, K. and Tate, A. O-plan: an overview of the open planning architecture. In M. Merry, editor, *BCS Expert Systems '85*, pages 225–240. British Computer Society Workshop Series, Cambridge University Press, Cambridge, England, 1985.

139 Meta-level Inference

The word "*Meta-X*" can be read as "*X about X*". So, for instance the word "*Meta-knowledge*" can be read as "*knowledge about knowledge*, the word "*meta-level*" as "*at a level about another level* and the word "*meta-level inference* as *inference performed at a level which is about another level*". More generally, when speaking of meta-level inference, we think of the following:

- There are two theories, one (usually called the *object theory*) which is about a given topic, and another one (usually called the *meta-theory*) which is about the object theory. The two theories may or may not in general share the same language.
- The inferences performed in the meta-theory are called *meta-level inferences*. In general, the process of carrying on deduction in the meta-theory is called "*meta-level inference*".

For instance,

- $x^2 - 3x + 2 = 0 \quad \rightarrow \quad x = 1$ or 2.
- $x^2 - 3x + 2 = 0$ contains two occurrences of the unknown 'x'.

are statements in respectively the theory and the meta-theory of algebra.

The goal of object-level inference is to obtain results in the topic of interest. The goal of meta-level inference is to obtain results about the theory of the topic of interest (the object theory) and then to use them to obtain *better results* about the topic of interest. Better results can mean "*to solve the problem in less time*" (in which case the meta-level inference is used to control or guide the search at the object level), "*to get results otherwise unavailable*" (in which case the meta-level inference is used to extend the solutions possibly obtainable by the object level) or "*to describe the object-level*" (in which case the meta-level inference is used to get a better understanding on the object level which can then be used for further operations, e.g. learning), and so on.

Contributors: Fausto Giunchiglia, Frank van Harmelen, and Robin Boswell.

Reference

Aiello, L. and Levi, G. The uses of metaknowledge in AI sytems. In *Proceedings of IJCAI-77*, pages 705-720. International Joint Conference on Artificial Intelligence, 1977.

140 Meta-rules

In the context of linguistics, meta-rules are a way of increasing the expressive power of a grammatical formalism. Informally, a grammar with meta-rules added provides two ways of including rules in a grammar - explicitly, by adding individual rules, or implicitly, by adding meta-rules. A meta-rule says 'If there is a rule of such-and-such a form in the grammar, then take the grammar as also containing another rule of such-and-such a form'.

Context-free grammars <**45**> are well suited to extension by meta-rules.

Contributor: Henry Thompson.

References

Gazdar, G. Phrase structure grammar. In P. Jacobson and G.K. Pullum, editors, *The Nature of Syntactic Representations*, pages 131–186. Reidel, Dordrecht, 1981.

Thompson, H.S. Handling metarules in a parser for GPSG. In M. Barlow, D. Flickinger, and I. Sag, editors, *Developments in Generalised Phrase Structure Grammar*, Bloomington, Indiana University Linguistics Club, 1982. Stanford Working Papers in Grammatical Theory Volume 2.

141 Minimax

Given a (partial) **game tree** <**8**> between Max and Min, with Max to play at the root of the tree. All leaf nodes have as immediate descendants the complete set of alternatives that can derive from that node. The leaf nodes of the tree are labelled with values, such that, the larger the value, the more favourable it is for Max. The Minimax value of such a tree is derived by starting at the leaf nodes and *backing up* values in the following manner. If the parent (P) of a set of sibling nodes (p_i) whose values are all know is Max, then P=max(p_i). If the parent is Min, then P=min(p_i). This procedure is recursive and results in eventually labelling the root node with a value. The optimal path through the tree from the point of view of both adversaries is know as the Maximin path.

Contributor: Hans Berliner.

Reference

Von Neumann, J. and Morgenstern, O. *The Theory of Games and Economic Behaviour.* John Wiley and Sons, New York, 1967.

142 Modal Logic

True propositions can be divided into those - such as "2+2=4" - which are necessarily true and those - such as "Mars has two moons" - which are contingently true. If "α" is some proposition then we write "$L\alpha$" (or $\Box\alpha$) to mean "α is necessarily true". We can define "$M\alpha$" (or $\Diamond\alpha$), read as "α is possibly true", as equivalent to "$\neg L \neg \alpha$". "L" and "M" are modal operators. A modal logic is an extension of standard logic obtained by adding to some version of standard logic the modal operators together with appropriate axioms and rules of inference. A great many system of modal logic have been constructed of which the most important are systems T, S4 and S5. The modal system T has as axioms some set of axioms appropriate to the standard propositional calculus together with:

$$L\alpha \rightarrow \alpha$$

$$L(\alpha \rightarrow \beta) \rightarrow (L\alpha \rightarrow L\beta)$$

We add to the rules of inference of our standard logic a **rule of necessitation** to the effect that if α is theorem then so is $L\alpha$. The system S4 is obtained by adding to T:

$$L\alpha \rightarrow LL\alpha$$

and S5 by adding to T:

$$M\alpha \rightarrow LM\alpha$$

Modal predicate logic can be obtained by making analogous additions to standard **predicate logic <180>**. To construct a model of one of the above systems we postulate a set of possible worlds W, an assignment of a truth value to each atomic formula for each world and a relation of accessibility between a particular world and a subset of W. "$L\alpha$" is true in a world in such a model if and only if it is true in every world accessible to that world in that model. A proposition is valid if and only if it is true in every such model. If we require that the accessibility relation be reflexive then the valid propositions are those provable in T. If we also require that the system be transitive then we get as valid the theorems of S4. Finally if we also require that the relation be symmetric we get as valid the theorems of S5.

Contributor: Colin Phillips.

Reference

Hughes, G.E. and Cresswell, M.J. *An Introduction to Modal Logic*, Methuen, London, 1972.

143 Model-Based Vision

A computer-vision technique in which interpretation of the image data is aided by some form of model of what is expected to be seen in the image. For example, a part inspection system would use a description (model) of where the key features of the part were and where specific tests should be undertaken. The main reasons for this approach are: (1) without some representation of the object no sensible identification is possible, (2) the use of a geometric model may allow one to infer the position of the object in the scene and (3) the model can be used to direct the image processing, thus saving considerable processing time.

The model may be implicit in the image analysis program, but more sophisticated approaches use explicitly defined models (allowing substitution of new models). The models may be expressed in many forms, including: geometric models (*e.g.* sizes and positional relationships between features), relational models (*e.g.* a graph with arcs representing pairwise relationships) or property models (*e.g.* a table of the expected properties, like area, color, etc.).

There is a fuzzy dividing line between the use of 'model-based' for specific objects or object classes, and the use of the term for more generic features, such as lines. That is, a model of a line, or a curve, is a generally useful model and may be as precise and explicit as a model of a real object. In these cases, one often uses the term 'knowledge-based' because these features are more abstract, and their identification usually depends more on knowledge of how they appear in an image.

Contributor: Robert B. Fisher

Reference

Fisher, R.B. *From Surfaces to Objects: Computer Vision and Three Dimensional Scene Analysis.* John Wiley and Sons, Chichester, 1989.

144 Model Matching

If an image contains an unknown object with f features, F_i of which are know to correspond to one of n known objects (models) M_j having m_j features, the problem of **matching** image features to model features can be expressed as an **interpretation tree** (IT). The root node of tree IT_j for model M_j has m_j descendants and the complete tree will have f levels. The total number of possible interpretations therefore is

$$\sum_{j=1}^{n}(m_j)^f$$

For even quite small numbers of features the interpretation tree quickly becomes too large to handle. Fortunately, very few interpretations in the tree are consistent with the data and by **pruning** those branches that are inconsistent the tree can be reduced to a more managable size. The constraints used include the distances between features, the angles between features and the sign of the triple product between corresponding surface normals.

Contributor: H.W. Hughes

Reference

Grimson, W.E.L. and Lozano-Perez, T. Model-Based Recognition and Localisation from Sparse Range or Tactile Data. *The International Journal of Robotics Research*, 3(3):3–35, 1984.

145 Modulation Transfer Function

A modulation transfer function is a description of a system's frequency response. It is a plot of the input to output amplitude ratio as a function of the frequency of the sinusoidally modulated input signal. See also **Fourier Transform <83>**.

Contributor: Jon Mayhew.

Reference

Campbell, F.W.C and Robson, J. Application of fourier analysis to the visibility of gratings. *J. Physiol. (Lond)*, 197:551–566, 1968.

146 Morphographemics

Alias: **spelling rules.**

The productivity of word-formation processes in many languages make it impossible to have every word in the lexicon. Systematic characterisation of the regularities in computationally exploitable fashion is the concern of computational morphographemics. The characterisation has to cover both combination and respelling constraints on word components. Simple ad hoc approaches to segmenting words so that their components can be looked up in the dictionary are fairly easy to devise for languages like English.

Contributor: Henry Thompson.

References

Kay, M. Morphological and syntactic analysis. In A. Zampolli, editor, *Linguistic Structures Processing*, pages 131–234. North Holland, Amsterdam and Oxford, 1977.

Kaplan, R.M. and Kay, M. *Word recognition.* Technical Report, Xerox Palo Alto Research Center, 1982.

Koskenniemi, K. Two-level model for morphological analysis. In A. Bundy, editor, *Proceedings of the IJCAI-83*, pages 683–685. International Joint Conference on Artificial Intelligence, W. Kaufmann, Los Altos, CA, 1983.

147 Multi-actor System

Alias: **multi-agent system.**

A multi-actor system is a combination of two or more **plan generation** and **plan execution** systems (actors) which act and intercommunicate in a shared task environment. **Communication actions** between actors (eg request for information, provision of information, provision of partial plan) may be handled as ordinary actions and are closely related to **speech acts** in natural language theory. Techniques have been devised whereby one actor's beliefs about the beliefs of another may be expressed and computed.

Note: this use of the term 'actor' is substantially different from that employed in the actor model of computation (see **actors <4>**).

Contributor: Jim Doran.

References

Thorndyke, P.W., McArthur D. and Cammarata, S. Autopilot: a distributed planner for airfleet control. In *Proceedings of IJCAI-81*, pages 171–177. International Joint Conference on Artificial Intelligence, W. Kaufmann, Los Altos, CA, 1981.

Wilks, Y. and Bien, J. *Beliefs, point of view and multiple environments.* CSCM-6, Colchester Cognitive Studies Centre, University of Essex, 1981.

148 Multi-pulse LPC

Alias: **modified linear predictive analysis, synthesis of speech, vocoder.**

An improved technique of **linear predictive coding** <128> in which the normal white noise or impulses excitation of the **linear predictive filter** is replaced by a modified impulse excitation only. A **perceptually weighted spectrum matching** technique is used to place the impulses.

Contributor: Andrew Varga.

Reference

Atal, B.S. and Remde, J.R. A new model of LPC excitation for producing natural sounding speech at low bit rates. In *Proc. IEEE ICASSP*, pages 614–617, 1982.

149 Naive Physics

Naive physics identifies the core knowledge underlying commonsense physical intuition and allows the modelling of **qualitative reasoning** <195> in explaining or predicting changes in the physical world. It is a logic-based theory based on qualitative concepts of physics and the intuitive knowledge that lay people bring to bear in attempting to make sense of their physical world and in predicting significant events in the state of that world. For example, Hayes gives a theory for liquids in first order logic; Allen and Kautz present a model of naive temporal reasoning for natural language comprehension and problem solving. Rather than descriptions of systems in terms of algebraic formulae and differential equations, naive physics seeks to expose causal relationships and to reason about changes in physical systems. For instance, consider a physical system consisting of a bath with both taps running and the plug inserted. Without building a quantitative model in terms of rate of water flow, volume of the bath, etc. naive physics can predict that the carpet will (eventually) get wet.

Contributor: Helen Lowe.

Reference

Hayes, P. The Naive Physics Manifesto. In J.R. Hobbs and R.C. Moore, editors, *Formal Theories of the Commonsense World.* Ablex Pub. Corp., Norwood, 1985.

150 Natural Deduction

Natural deduction is a formal inference system which is said naturally to mirror the way in which humans reason. A natural deduction system consists of rules of inference eliminating and introducing each of the connectives and quantifiers of the **Predicate Calculus <180>**. There are twelve rules which may be used to infer conclusions. Two examples of such rules are given below:

$$\frac{A \qquad A \to B}{B} \qquad\qquad \frac{\begin{matrix}\overline{A}\\ | \\ B\end{matrix}}{A \to B}$$

The rule on the left is that to eliminate the $\to$ connective and that on the right to introduce it.

Natural deduction proofs are trees, the leaves representing the assumptions, and the root, the conclusion that has been deduced from those assumptions. It is valid in natural deduction to assume temporarily certain formulae, and then 'discharge' these assumptions later in the proof, by using certain of the deduction rules. The $\to$ Introduction rule above is an example of a rule which discharges an assumption (A in this case). Natural deduction is sound and complete.

Contributor: Dave Plummer.

References

Prawitz, D. *Natural Deduction.* Almquist and Wiksell, Stockholm, 1965

Tennant, N. *Natural Logic.* Edinburgh University Press, Edinburgh, 1978.

151 Negation as Failure

Negation as failure is a **rule of inference** which allows one to deduce that NOT P is true if all possible proofs of P fail.

This is the way that negation is treated in **Prolog <187>** and **Micro-PLANNER**. When using a system for database access, the assumption that negation as failure corresponds to true negation is precisely a consequence of the **Closed World Assumption** i.e. the assumption that all relevant information is contained in the database. Without the Closed World Assumption, negation as failure corresponds to 'we assume something is false if we cannot deduce it from available information', which is not the same as true negation. Negation as failure is an example of **default reasoning <54>**. It's mathematical meaning is extremely questionable .

Contributor: Martin Merry.

References

Clark, K.L. Negation as failure. In H. Gallaire and J. Minker, editors, *Logic and DataBases*, pages 293–322. Plenum Press, New York and London, 1978.

Reiter, R. On closed world databases. In H. Gallaire and J. Minker, editors, *Logic and DataBases*, pages 55–76. Plenum Press, New York and London, 1978.

152 Neighbourhood Parallelism

The technique of using immediate parallel access to the whole set of locations that form the neighbourhood of an operation. This may be restricted to a single bit plane. See **cellular arrays <31>**.

Contributors: T P Pridmore, S R Pollard, S T Stenton.

Reference

Danielsson, P. and Levialdi, S. Computer architectures for pictorial information systems. *IEEE Computer*, 53–67, November 1981.

153 Noise Reduction

Alias: **Noise Smoothing**

Imaging devices produce a certain amount of noise, that is a random signal which does not carry any useful information. If the amplitude of the noise is higher than the amplitude of the signal that is to be analysed, the information cannot be directly extracted from the noisy signal. However, it is often the case that most of the noise energy is concentrated in high spatial frequencies (see **Fourier transforms <83>**). If the signal to be extracted carries most of its information in lower spatial frequencies, it is possible to use a low pass filter (smoothing filter) which damps the higher frequencies. Then it is possible to extract the required information better.

Filtering is performed by convolving an image with a mask which is adapted to the task it should perform. Its shape can be determined exactly if the statistical distribution of the spectral components of signal and noise is known (**Wiener filter**). For simple low pass filters one often uses masks which approximate a Gaussian in section. Simple masks like equal valued discs blur the image, but do not damp high frequencies as effectively as a **Gaussian mask**.

Contributor: Fritz Seytter

Reference

Pratt, W.K. *Digital image processing.* Wiley, New York and Chichester, 1978

154 Non-linear Planning

Alias: **partially-ordered plans, parallel planning**

Non-linear planners are able to maintain the emerging plan as a partially-ordered network of actions. Unnecessary ordering (or linearisation) of the actions is avoided. Only when there are conflicts between parallel branches of the plan (such as the inability to determine a required condition at some point) is an ordering imposed. The first such system was Sacerdoti's **NOAH**.

A complete treatment of the handling of alternatives and all legal linearisations after an interaction between **subgoals <233>** is detected was included in Tate's **NONLIN**. The ability to use the same technique in the presence of time constraints on particular actions was a feature of Vere's **DEVISER**. Most non-linear planners also use **hierarchical planning** techniques.

Contributor: Austin Tate.

References

Sacerdoti, E.D. *A structure for plans and behaviour.* Elsevier North-Holland, New York, 1977.

Tate, A. Generating project networks. In *Proceedings of IJCAI-77*, pages 888-893. International Joint Conference on Artificial Intelligence, 1977.

Vere, S.A. Planning in time: windows and durations for activities and goals. *IEEE Trans. on Pattern Analysis and Machine Intelligence*, 5(3):246–267, 1983.

155 Non-monotonic Reasoning

Alias: **non-monotonic logic**

Non-monotonic logics deal with non-monotonic reasoning; this is reasoning that involves adopting assumptions that may have to be abandoned in the light of new information. This reasoning is called non-monotonic in contrast with the monotonicity of deductive logic, in which the addition of new axioms to a set of axioms can never decrease the set of theorems or facts; quite often the new axioms give rise to new theorems so that the set of theorems grows monotonically with the set of axioms. In non-monotonic logics, the set of theorems may lose members as well as gain members when new axioms are added.

Non-monotonicity is a common feature of ordinary reasoning. For instance, if we are told that Tweety is a bird we assume (s)he can fly, but withdraw this when we are told that (s)he is a penguin; this **default reasoning <54>** is a way of overcoming the problem of insufficient information; the system is told that unless it has information to the contrary certain defaults are assumed to be true.

Examples of systems utilising default reasoning are **Thnot** in **PLANNER** and the **negation as failure <151>** of **Prolog <187>**. In the latter the system assumes that if it has not been told that a certain fact is true then it is false: this is the so-called **closed world assumption.** See also **Truth maintenance system <245>**, **Default Logic <54>**, and **Circumscription <34>**.

Contributor: Luis Jenkins and Dave Plummer.

References

Special issue on non-monotonic logic. *Artificial Intelligence*, Vol.13, 1981.

Ginsberg, M.L. *Readings in Non-monotonic Reasoning.* Morgan Kaufmann, Los Altos, California, 1987.

156 Numerically-controlled Machine Tools

A machine tool is a power-driven machine for cutting, grinding, drilling, or otherwise shaping a metal workpiece. A numerically-controlled (NC) machine tool is a system in which actions are controlled by numerical data given by a program. The program can position a tool point in three dimensions relative to a workpiece, and can control other function such as speed, coolant flow, gaging, and selection of tools. Most NC tools can be programmed in the **APT** language with **FORTRAN <81>** subroutines. The capability to perform 3D geometrical calculations makes it possible to sculpt arbitrarily complicated shapes. **Sensory feedback <215>** is used to report differences between actual and desired tool movements, and between actual and desired workpiece dimensions to cause the NC tool to correct or minimise the error. This can automatically compensate for tool wear and detect tool breakage. Robot manipulators can be used to feed blank workpieces and to remove finished ones.

Contributor: W.F. Clocksin.

References

Simon, W. *The Numerical Control of Machine Tools.* Edward Arnold, 1978.

Faux, I.D. and Pratt, M.J. *Computational Geometry for Design and Manufacture.* Ellis Horwood, Chichester, 1979.

157 Object-centred Co-ordinates

An object is described in object-centred co-ordinates if the coordinate origin is fixed with respect to the object, the coordinate axes are defined by the structure of the object, and all other object points are defined with respect to that system. This description is, then, independent of viewpoint. One task of a vision system is to move from **viewer-centered description <252>** to object-centered description.

Contributors: T P Pridmore, S R Pollard, S P Stenton.

Reference

Marr, D. *Vision: a computational investigaion into the human representation and processing of visual information.* W.H. Freeman, New York, 1982.

158 One-Then-Best Backtracking

Since there is often good local information available to indicate the preferred solution path, it is often best to try out that indicated by heuristic information before considering the many alternatives that may be available should the local choice prove faulty. Taken to the extreme, **Depth-first Search <61>** gives something of the flavour of such a search strategy. However, gradual wandering from a valid solution path could entail backtracking through many levels when a failure is detected.

An alternative is to focus on the choice currently being made and try to select one of the local choices which seems most promising. This continues while all is going well (perhaps with some cut-off points to take a long, hard look at how well things are going). However, if a failure occurs, the *whole* set of alternatives which have been generated (and ranked by a heuristic evaluator) are reconsidered to select a re-focussing point for the search. Such a search strategy is used in Tate's NONLIN, for example.

Contributor: Austin Tate.

Reference

Tate, A. *Project Planning using a Hierarchic Non-linear Planner.* Research Report 25, Department of Artificial Intelligence, Edinburgh University, 1975.

159 Operators

Alias: **operator schema, action schema**

In the context of planning, **operators** represent the (generic) actions which the actor can execute in the planning environment. Operators are commonly represented as three lists: a list of **preconditions**, a list of facts that will be true after application of the operator (ADD LIST) and a list of facts that will no longer be true after the operator is applied (DELETE LIST). These lists normally involve variables which must be bound for any particular instance of the action.

The difficulty encountered in fully capturing the effects of actions in non-trivial planning domains using such operators is an aspect of the **frame problem.**

Contributors: Maarten van Someren and Jim Doran.

Reference

Nilsson, N.J. *Principles of Artificial Intelligence.* Tioga Pub. Co., Palo Alto, California, 1980.

```
,-------------------------------,
| Preconditions   | operator 01  |
:-----------------------------------------------,
| 01's PRECOND    | 01's ADD LIST | operator 02   |
:---------------------------------------------------------------,
| 02's  PRECOND,  | facts in cell | 02's ADD LIST |               |
| not in this row | above minus   |               | operator 03   |
|                 | DELETE 02     |               |               |
:---------------------------------------------------------------:
| 03's PRECOND,   | facts in cell | facts in cell | 03's ADD LIST |
| not in this row | above minus   | above minus   |               |
|                 | DELETE 03     | DELETE 03     |               |
`---------------------------------------------------------------'
```

160 Operator Tables

Alias: **triangle table, MACROPS.**

When **macro operators <133>** are built from elementary **operators <159>**, the original operators and the macro operator are available, but not any subsequences of the macro operator. For example, if O(20) was built from O(1) through O(10), then it is not possible to use the subsequence O(8) through O(10). The representation in the figure accompanying this entry was devised to overcome this inefficiency.

Facts that are preconditions for an operator are marked in each cell. To reach a goal state, the program looks for a row in the table that contains the facts of the goal state. The operator of the row above is the last operator to be applied. Next, it moves back until an operator is found for which all preconditions are currently true. This is the first operator to be applied.

A triangular table like the one above may be produced as a result of a solution process. This will reduce search on future problems. The macro operators should be generalised (with respect to variable bindings) if they are to be of any use.

Contributor: Maarten van Someren.

Reference

Fikes, R.E., Hart, P.E. and Nilsson, N.J. Learning and executing generalised robot plans. *Artificial Intelligence*, 3:251–288, 1972.

161 Opportunistic Search

Some systems do not have a fixed (goal-driven <93> or **data-driven** <51>) directional approach to solving a problem. Instead a current 'focus' for the search is identified on the basis of the most constrained way forwards. This may be suggested by comparison of the current goals with the initial world model state, by consideration of the number of likely outcomes of making a selection, by the degree to which goals are instantiated, etc. Any problem-solving component may summarise its requirements for the solution as constraints on possible solutions or restrictions of the values of variables representing objects being manipulated. It can then suspend its operations until further information becomes available on which a more definite choice can be made.

Many such systems operate with a **Blackboard** <20> through which the various components can communicate via constraint information. The scheduling of the various tasks associated with arriving at a solution may also be dealt with through the blackboard.

Contributor: Austin Tate.

References

Hayes, P.J. A representation for robot plans. In *Proceedings of IJCAI-75*, pages 181–188. International Joint Conference on Artificial Intelligence, 1975.

Hayes-Roth, B. and Hayes-Roth, F. A cognitive model of planning. *Cognitive Science*, 3:275–310, 1979.

Stallman, R.M. and Sussman, G.J. Forward-reasoning and dependency-directed backtracking. *Artificial Intelligence*, 9:135–196, 1977.

162 Optical Flow

The instantaneous positional relative velocity field of a scene projected onto an imaginary surface : a retinal velocity map. Mathematical analysis has shown that from a monocular view of a rigid, textured, curved surface it is possible to determine the gradient of the surface at any point and the motion relative to that surface from the velocity field of the changing retinal image and its first and second spatial derivatives. See **intrinsic images <113>**.

Contributors: T P Pridmore, S R Pollard, S T Stenton.

Reference

Longuet-Higgens, H.C. and Prazdny, K. The interpretation of moving retinal images. *Proc. R. Soc. London*, B208:385–387, 1980.

163 Optimistic Plan Execution

When a **plan structure <175>** is executed, there is no guarantee that the sequence of planning environment states predicted by the plan will actually occur. Deviation from expectation due to faulty planning or faulty **operator <159>** execution is very likely.

When an optimistic plan execution technique executes an operator in a plan and so encounters a new environment state, it attempts to identify the new state by matching it successively against all the states predicted in the plan, working backwards from the goal. The first match found determines which operator in the plan is to be executed next. If no match is found, then replanning is needed.

The advantage of this somewhat laborious technique is that the execution of unnecessary operators may be avoided and some execution failures can be overcome by repeating the execution of operators.

Contributor: Jim Doran.

Reference

Fikes, R.E., Hart, P.E. and Nilsson, N.J. Learning and executing generalised robot plans. *Artificial Intelligence*, 3:251–288, 1972.

164 Paramodulation

A **rule of inference** of **predicate calculus** <**180**>, used to deduce a new formula from two old ones. It is used in **automatic theorem proving**, in conjunction with **resolution** <**204**>, as an alternative to the axioms of equality. All the three formulae involved must be in **clausal form** <**36**>. If $C[t']$ and D are **clauses**, where $C[t']$ indicates that C contains a particular occurrence of t'. then the rule is

$$\frac{C[t'] \qquad D \vee s = t}{(C[s] \vee D)\theta} \qquad\qquad \frac{C[t'] \qquad D \vee t = s}{(C[s] \vee D)\theta}$$

where θ is the most general **unifier** of t and t', and is obtained by **unification** <**248**>. $C[s]$ indicates that only the particular occurrence of t' is replaced by s in C, other occurrences of t' are untouched.

Contributor: Alan Bundy.

Reference

Chang, C. and Lee, R.C. *Symbolic Logic and Mechanical Theorem Proving.* Academic Press, New York, 1973.

165 Partial Evaluation

The main goal of partial evaluation is to perform as much of the computation in a program as possible by using a partial specification of the input values of the program. The theoretical foundation for partial evaluation is Kleene's S-M-N theorem from **recursive function theory** <**197**>.

The partial evaluation algorithm takes as its input a function (program) definition, together with a partial specification of the input of the program, and produces a new version of the program that is specialised for the particular input values. The new version of the program will then be less general but more efficient then the original version.

The partial evaluation algorithm works by symbolically evaluating the input program while in the mean time trying to 1) propagate constant values through the program code, 2) unfold procedure calls, and 3) branching out conditional parts of the code. If the input program is logical, then the symbolic evaluation of the program becomes the construction of the proof tree corresponding to the execution of the program.

In recent years partial evaluation in **Logic Programming <131>** has attracted particular attention in connection with meta-programming as an optimisation technique.

Contributor: Frank van Harmelen.

References

Futuram, Y. Partial evaluation of computation process – an approach to a compiler–compiler. *Systems, Computers, Controls*, 25:45–50, 1971.

Komorowski, H.J. *A specification of an Abstract Prolog Machine and its Application to Partial Evaluation.* PhD thesis, Technical Report LSST 69, Linkoping University, 1981.

Bjoner, D., Ershov, A.P. and Jones, N.D. (editors). *Proceedings of the workshop on partial evaluation and mixed computation*, G. Avernaes, Denmark, October 1987. North Holland and New Generation Computing Journal, 1988

166 Partitioned Semantic Net

Means of enhancing the organisational and expressive power of **semantic nets <213>** through the grouping of nodes and links, associated with Hendrix. Nodes and links may figure in one or more '**spaces**', which may themselves be bundled into higher-level '**vistas**', which can be exploited autonomously and structured hierarchically. The effective encoding of logical statements involving **connectives** and **quantifiers** was an important motivation for partitioning, but the partitioning mechanisms involved are sufficiently well-founded, general and powerful to support the dynamic representation of a wide range of language and world knowledge; and partitioned nets have been extensively used for a range of such purposes at SRI.

Contributor: Karen Sparck Jones.

Reference

Hendrix, G.G. Encoding knowledge in partitioned networks. In N.V. Findler, editor, *Associative Networks*, pages 51-92. Academic Press, New York, 1979.

167 Pattern Directed Languages

This class of languages is **data-driven** <51>. That is, the current context is used to determine which procedure to call next —sometimes called **pattern directed invocation** <168>. This is opposed to the fixed sequence of procedure calls in languages like **FORTRAN** <81>, **ALGOL** etc. There is a corresponding necessity for suitable **pattern matching** <169> to take place.

Examples languages include **PLANNER** (and **Micro-PLANNER**), **CONNIVER**, **QLISP** (and **QA4**), **Prolog** <187> and **Production Rule Systems** <184> like **OPS5**.

Different styles of reasoning are possible: **OPS5**, for example, uses **forward chaining** <82> while **Prolog** uses **backwards chaining** <13>. Also, different styles of pattern matching are used: **PLANNER** uses an extremely simple algorithm while **QLISP** can match pattern variables to arbitrary **Lisp** <129> structures.

The problem of **conflict resolution** also arises when, in principle, one pattern is suitable for several different procedure invocations. This is solved in

Prolog by using a fixed search strategy and in **OPS5** with a simple conflict resolution algorithm.

Contributor: Paul Brna

Reference

Waterman, D.A. and Hayes-Roth, F. (editors). *Pattern-directed Inference Systems.* Academic Press, New York. 1978.

168 Pattern Directed Retrieval/Invocation

The retrieval of a datum from a **database** by virtue of its syntactic form. A **pattern** (or template) of the required datum is compared with the data in the database; data that 'match' with the pattern are retrieved. A successful match may bind the unspecified parts (variables) of either or both of the pattern and 'target' datum. In the case of procedure invocation, a pattern is associated with each procedure. Calls to a procedure are made when the current situation or goal matches the associated pattern of the procedure. This allows for a more flexible control flow as procedures are not called by name but by content. This form of retrieval/invocation is central to the **PLANNER** type languages; two way **Pattern Matching** <**169**> (or **unification** <**248**>) being the basis of the **resolution** <**204**> principle on which **Prolog** <**187**> is based.

Contributor: Lincoln Wallen.

Reference

Waterman, D.A. and Hayes-Roth, F. (editors). *Pattern directed inference systems.* Academic Press, New York, 1978.

169 Pattern Matching

In its most general form a pervasive feature of, or basis for, AI systems: the essential objective is to test whether a specific received data structure is an instance of a given general pattern, and particularly, to establish whether input data items can provide values for **pattern variables**. The matching can be made more or less fuzzy, according to the conditions on the individual pattern variables, and on their joint satisfaction. Pattern matching is important in AI because it reflects (a) the fact that complex general concepts exhibit considerable variation in particular manifestations, and (b) the fact that individual elements of these participate in relationships with one another. See also **Unification<248>**.

Contributor: Karen Sparck Jones.

170 Perceptrons

A parallel decision making mechanism that superficially resembles the sort of processing that may be characteristic of neurons in the brain. It is a pattern recognition device with a threshold. If the linear combination of the 'weighted inputs' is greater than some threshold value then the perceptron 'fires'. It is possible for a perceptron to learn, eg, if the weights associated with the inputs that were active in the case of a false alarm are decreased, and weights associated with inputs that were active in the case of a miss are increased then it is intuitively plausible that recognition performance will improve. There is a theorem that says that a perceptron will learn to recognise a class correctly over a finite number of errors. The analysis of the mathematical properties of perceptrons revealed profound limitations to their competence. These limitations are largely due to the difficulties inherent in making global decisions on the basis of only local evidence. Thus a perceptron can't tell whether a figure is connected or not, or whether there is one, and only one, instance of a pattern present. Nevertheless there is a resurgence of interest in perceptrons associated with the development of **connectionist schemes** for visual processing. See **connectionism <40>**.

Contributor: Jon Mayhew.

171 Photometric Stereo

A technique for recovering shape information from **reflectance maps <198>**. Given an image and a reflectance map for one light source, the intensity at a particular image location constrains the surface orientation to lie on a contour in the reflectance map. If three images are taken with different light source positions the surface orientation must lie on a known contour in each of the three associated reflectance maps, hence the intersection of these contours specifies the surface orientation.

Contributors: T P Pridmore, S R Pollard, S T Stenton.

Reference

Marr, D. *Vision: a computational investigaion into the human representation and processing of visual information.* W.H. Freeman, New York, 1982.

172 Pipelining

An architecture suitable for repeating the same series of operations on different data in an operator parallel fashion. The data stream flows through the pipeline of operations, each data item being at a different stage of serial processing. The operations take place in parallel, their results being passed on to the next operation. Computational efficiency is equivalent to that of performing the whole task at the rate of the most complex sub-operation. Thus the more complex and partitioned the task the more suitable it is for pipelining.

Contributors: T P Pridmore, S R Pollard, S T Stenton.

Reference

Danielsson, P. and Levialdi, S. Computer architectures for pictorial information systems. *IEE Computer*, 53–67, November 1981.

173 Pitch Extraction

There are three main algorithms used for performing pitch extraction for speech synthesis and recognition: the Gold-Rabiner parallel processing method with voiced-unvoiced decision, the Dubnowski autocorrelation method and the Harmonic-sieve pitch extraction method.

Contributor: Andrej Ljolje.

References

Gold, B. and Rabiner, L. Parallel processing techniques for estimating pitch periods of speech in the time domain. *JASA*, 46(2):442, 1969.

Gold, B. Note on buzz-hiss detection. *JASA*, 36(9):1659, 1964.

Dubnowski, J.J., Schafer, R.W. and Rabiner, L.R. Real-time digital hardware pitch detector. *IEEE Trans. ASSP*, 24(1):2, 1976.

Duifhuis, H., Willems, L.F. and Sluyter, R.J. Measurement of pitch in speech: an implementation of Goldstein's theory of pitch perception. *JASA*, 71(6):1568, 1982.

174 Plan Recognition

Alias: **plan inference**.

Given a sequence of actions carried out in a task domain by some actor, it is possible to draw conclusions about the plan that the actor is executing by working bottom up. If the actor's top goal is known or can be guessed, then a top down matching process is feasible. The task of plan recognition can be related to chart parsing <**33**> and can be partially formalised using a first order theory of action and **circumscription** <**34**>.

Contributor: Jim Doran.

References

Schmidt, C.F., Sridharan, N.S. and Goodson, J.L. The plan recognition problem. *Artificial Intelligence*, 11:45–83, 1978.

Allen, J. and Perrault, C. Analyzing intention in utterances. *Artificial Intelligence*, 15:143–178, 1980.

175 Plan Structure

A plan structure embodies a partially or totally ordered set of partially instantiated **operators <159>** together with the (sub) goals to which they are directed, and information which indicates how the planning environment is predicted to change as the plan is executed. Plan structure can be contrasted with **Goal Structure <93>**, as used in **operator tables <160>** where the purposes of the plan's parts are recorded.

Contributor: Jim Doran.

Reference

Nilsson, N.J. *Principles of Artificial Intelligence.* Tioga Pub. Co., Palo Alto, California, 1980.

176 Postulating Intrinsic Properties

Given two symbolic independent variables X and Y, and one numeric dependent variable Z, one cannot find a numeric law relating these terms (since only one is numeric). However, suppose that by holding X constant and varying Y, one observes different values for Z. Then one can postulate an intrinsic property I whose values are set to those of Z, and one can associate these numeric values with the symbolic values of Y. Since one now has two numeric terms Z and I, one can find the law $Z/I = 1.0$ (which is true tautologically). However, when a new value of X is examined and the same values of Y are used, one can retrieve the intrinsic values associated with Y. In this new context the ratio Z/I may take on some other constant value, which is an empirically meaningful law. This method can be used to infer intrinsic properties such as mass, specific heat, and the index of refraction from combinations of symbolic and numeric observations.

Contributor: Pat Langley.

References

Langley, P., Bradshaw, G. and Simon, H.A. Rediscovering chemistry with the bacon system. In R. Michalski, J. Carbonell, and

T. Mitchell, editors, *Machine Learning: An Artificial Intelligence View.* Tioga Pub. Co., Palo Alto, California, 1983.

Bradshaw, G., Langley, P. and Simon, H.A. The discovery of intrinsic properties. In *Proc. of the Third Nat. Conf.*, Canadian Soc for Computational Studies of Intelligence, 1980.

177 Precondition Analysis

Precondition Analysis is an analytic strategy-learning technique. Preconditions Analysis operates in two phases: the learning cycle and the performance cycle. In the learning cycle, the program is given an example of a correctly executed task.

The example may contain several individual steps, each step being the application of an **operator <159>**. The program first examines the example, to find out which operators were used in performing the task. This stage is called Operator Identification. During this phase, the program may discover that it doesn't possess the relevant operator, and the user is asked to provide the necessary information.

Once this phase is complete the program builds an explanation of the strategic reasons for each step of the task. The explanation is in terms of satisfying the preconditions of following steps.

From this explanation, it builds a plan that is used by the performance element. These plans are called schemas. The performance element executes the schemas in a flexible way, using the explanation to guide it. The explanations are used to make sensible patches if the plan can't be used directly.

Precondition Analysis has been implemented in LP (Learning PRESS), a program that learns new techniques for solving algebraic equations. Precondition Analysis is somewhat similar to the Explanation-Based Generalisation approach of Mitchell, but differs in that Precondition Analysis can work in domains in which the methods are not invertible, and in situations where the domain theory is imperfect.

Contributor: Bernard Silver.

References

Silver, B. Learning equation solving methods from examples. In A. Bundy, editor, *Proceedings of IJCAI-83*, pages 429–431, International Joint Conference on Artificial Intelligence, 1983.

Silver, B. Precondition analysis: learning equation solving strategies from worked examples. In R.S. Michalski, J.G. Carbonell and T.M. Mitchell (editors), *Machine Learning: An Artificial Intelligence Approach*, Vol. 2. Tioga Pub. Co., Palo Alto, California, 1986.

178 Predictive Parsing

Alias: **expectation-based parsing.**

Predictive parsing is an approach to natural language analysis based on the use of powerful programs associated primarily with individual lexical items which embody expectations about the form and content of the subsequent sentence/text input. The expectations are intended to determine the analysis of further inputs by providing semantic structures into which they must fit. (These structures may be those of **preference semantics <181>**, **conceptual dependency <38>**, or, by generalisation, **scripts <209>**.) The essentially word-driven basis, and emphasis on semantic rather than syntactic information and processing, of this style of parsing makes it predictive in a very different sense from that of classical top-down syntactic parsing; and allowing the exploitation of any type or piece of information in a word program offers great flexibility. The price includes a lack of generality, and overlaps or gaps between individual programs. The approach is therefore best suited to domain-limited language processing.

The main application of expectation-based parsing has been in the extraction of conceptual dependency structures from English; the technique has also been generalised in the direct application of scripts to parsing. Word expert **parsing** is a specialisation of this approach confined to word-based expectations, but not restricted to left-to-right operation.

Contributor: Karen Sparck Jones.

Reference

Birnbaum, L. and Selfridge, M. Conceptual analysis of natural language. In R.C. Schank and C.K. Riesbeck, editors, *Inside Computer Understanding*, pages 318–353. Lawrence Erlbaum Associates, Hillsdale, New Jersey, 1981.

179 Principle of Least Commitment

This principle asserts that decisions should be deferred as long as possible before being taken, so that when they are taken the probability of their correctness is maximised. In the planning context, the principle is used to justify deferring action ordering decisions, and object choice decisions during plan elaboration. A consequence is an emphasis on the posting and propagation of constraints <**43**> that an object must satisfy.

Contributor: Jim Doran

References

Sacerdoti, E.D. *A structure for plans and behaviour.* Elsevier North-Holland, New York, 1977.

Stefik, M.J. Planning with constraints (Molgen: part 1). *Artificial Intelligence*, 16:111-139, 1981.

180 Predicate Calculus

Alias: **predicate logic**, **first-order logic**.

Predicate calculus is a formal language in which it is possible to express statements about simple domains. It comprises a set of symbols, and rules for combining these into terms and formulae. There are also rules of **inference**, which state how a new formula can be derived from old formulae. A logical system will have an initial set of sentences ('**axioms**') and any sentence which can be derived from these axioms using the inference rules is called a '**theorem**' of the system.

The standard logic is a well-defined notation in which exact descriptive statements can be formulated about any 'model' (i.e. set of objects with relations between them). Moreover, purely formal manipulations of these symbolic statements (i.e. inference) can be used to produce further valid descriptions of that same model, without direct reference to the model itself.

Terms can be constants (names of objects), variables (marking which part of a formula is quantified) or functions applied to arguments (e.g. $f(a,b,x)$). Atomic sentences are formed by applying a predicate to a set argument term (e.g. $\mathrm{P}(f(a,b,x),c,g(h(y)))$. Compound sentences can be formed by adding negation to a sentence (e.g. $\neg\mathrm{R}(a,b)$), joining two statements with a **connective** such as $\wedge$ ("and"), $\vee$ ("or"), $\rightarrow$ ("implication").

There are two **quantifiers** which, used together with variables, allow the expression of universal statements:

$(\forall x)\mathrm{Q}(x)$: "for all x, Q(x)"

and existential statements:

$(\exists z)\mathrm{R}(z,a)$: "there exists a z such that R(z,a)"

Automatic inference techniques (e.g. **resolution <204>**) for first-order logic have been widely explored.

Contributor: Graeme Ritchie.

References

Chang, C.C. and Keisler, A.J. *Model Theory.* North-Holland, Amsterdam and Oxford, 1937.

Crossley, J.N. et al. *What is Mathematical Logic?* Oxford University Press, Oxford, 1972.

181 Preference Semantics

An approach to language understanding most fully developed by Wilks. Preference semantics recognises that, in general, semantic constraints on word combinations cannot be absolute, as this would be incompatible with the creativity of language. The semantic patterns embodied e.g. in **case frames <30>**, and expressed e.g. by **semantic primitives <214>** indicate the mutual contextual preferences of words: for example 'hit' meaning STRIKE prefers a HUMAN Agent. Wilkes' special contribution was a preference metric, minimising information in the interpretation selected. Thus word sense and sentence structure selection in text processing is then determined by maximum constraint satisfaction, and does not depend on complete satisfaction. Analogously, where interpretation involves inference, the metric selects the interpretation depending on the shortest inference chain.

Contributor: Karen Sparck Jones.

Reference

Wilks, Y.A. A preferential, pattern seeking semantics for natural language inference. *Artificial Intelligence*, 6:53–74, 1975.

182 Primal Sketch

A term used by Marr for a representation making explicit the properties of intensity changes in the retinal image(s). The Raw Primal Sketch makes explicit only very localised properties, such as size, position and orientation; the Full Primal Sketch, resulting from grouping elements of the Raw Primal Sketch, makes explicit more global properties such as alignment. Marr claimed that higher level processes interact only with the primal sketch and its derivatives, not with the data from which the primal sketch is derived. The primal sketch is computed by dedicated processors which are independent of higher level processes.

Contributors: T P Pridmore, S R Pollard, S P Stenton.

Reference

Marr, D. *Vision: a computational investigaion into the human representation and processing of visual information.* W.H. Freeman, New York, 1982.

183 Procedural Attachment

Alias: **procedural embedding.**

It is often necessary in knowledge representation for an executable procedure to be directly associated with one or more data structures in order to indicate when it should be used. Attached procedures lie dormant until certain conditions are satisfied, at which point they are executed. In **KRL**, for example, two types of attached procedures were identified (but these hold for most systems):

- **servants**: these are executed when a procedure is required to apply some operation to a data object (or set of data objects), a selection mechanism may be required to select the correct procedure if more than one servant is available.
- **demons** <57>: these are invoked when something has been done or is about to be done, (note that all demons whose conditions are met are activated).

Two methods of attachment were identified:

- **traps**: these are procedures attached to individual data objects and apply to operations and events involving the unit to which they are attached.
- **triggers**: these are procedures attached to classes of data objects and apply to operations and events involving any objects in the class to which they are attached.

Both traps and triggers may be either servants or demons (c.f 'methods' in **CONNIVER** and 'theorems' in **Micro-PLANNER**).

Contributor: Robert Corlett.

Reference

Bobrow, D.G. and Winograd, T. An overview of KRL, a knowledge representation language. *Cognitive Science*, 1:3–46, 1977.

184 Production Rule System

Alias: **Production System, if/then rules, situation/action rules.**

A programming language in which the programs consist of condition => action rules. The programs are interpreted by a repetition of the following operations: all rules whose conditions are satisfied are found, one of them is selected, and its action is called. Such systems have been extensively used in computational psychology and knowledge engineering.

Contributor: Alan Bundy.

Reference

Newell, A. and Simon, H.A. *Human Problem Solving.* Prentice Hall, Englewood Cliffs, 1972.

185 Program Transformation

A technique for developing programs. An initial specification is written as a (probably inefficient) program and then transformed to an efficient version using methods guaranteed to preserve the meaning of the program. Within the **declarative languages** program transformations can be based on a small set of provably correct basic transformations facilitating the development of semi-automatic transformation systems.

Contributor: John Darlington.

186 Programming Cliche

Alias: **Idiom.**

Inspection methods are problem solving techniques which rely upon recognising the form of a solution. In programming there is a set of standard forms from which a wide range of programs can be constructed. This set of standard forms includes such things as particular control strategies with unspecified primitive actions. Such standard forms are know as programming cliches. The term originates from the MIT Programmer's Apprentice project. As a result of being more abstract, programming cliches are much more adaptable concepts than macros or subroutines.

Contributor: Kevin Poulter.

References

Rich, C. and Waters, R.C. *Abstraction, Inspection and Debugging in Programming.* AI Memo 634, MIT AI Lab., June 1981.

Perlis, A.J. and Rugaber, S. Programming with idioms in APL. In *APL79 Conf. Proc. and Rochester N.Y.*, 1979.

187 Prolog

Prolog is a programming language originally developed by Colmerauer around 1972. It can be seen as an attempt at a pure **logic programming <131>** language as it is based on the clausal form of first order predicate logic restricted to **Horn clauses <36>**. Essentially, it is a **resolution theorem prover <204>**.

Since the influential implementation of Prolog by D. H. Warren in 1976 and his development of the Warren Abstract Machine (WAM), Prolog has become more suitable for large programming tasks. Its adoption at the heart of the Japanese Fifth Generation Computer Systems project has led to an increase in the volume of research and development work worldwide.

Contributor: P Brna

References

Clocksin, W.F. and Mellish, C.S. *Programming in Prolog*, second edition. Springer Verlag, Berlin, 1984.

Sterling, L. and Shapiro, E.Y. *The Art of Prolog.* MIT Press, Cambridge, Mass., 1986.

188 Propagation in Cellular Arrays

One particular facet of the use of parallel cellular arrays for image processing is that the physical interconnection structure of the array can reflect the supposed connectivity of images. This approach is most useful when the array allows 'global propagation'. That is propagation of signals from pixel groups across arbitrary distances, with each intermediate **pixel** transforming the signal according to its local data. For example global propagation allows a **CLIP** series machine to extract a labelled component of a binary image of arbitrary complexity in one machine cycle. See also **relaxation labelling <203>** and **cellular arrays <31>**.

Contributor: Dave Reynolds.

Reference

Otto, G.P. *Counting and Labelling Objects on CLIP4.* Report 82/11, Image Processing Group, Dept. of Physics and Astronomy, University College London, 1982.

189 Property Lists

A technique whereby a list of name-value pairs is associated with an object (such as a node of a **semantic net <213>**). Each name represents a certain attribute of the object and the corresponding value records the value of that attribute assigned to the object. Such a facility for associating property lists with atoms is provided as a primitive operation in **Lisp** <**129**> type languages.

Contributor: Lincoln Wallen.

Reference

Allen, J. *Anatomy of LISP*. McGraw-Hill, New York, 1978.

190 Propositional Constraint Propagation

A propositional constraint is a **resolution** clause all of whose atoms are simple sentential variables. Propositional constraint propagation is an incomplete inference procedure which operates on propositional constraints and is equivalent to unit clause **resolution** <**204**>.

Contributor: D. McAllester.

Reference

McAllester, D. *An Outlook on Truth Maintenance*. AI Memo 551, MIT AI Lab., Cambridge, Mass., August 1980.

191 Protocol Analysis

A technique for extracting the procedures used by a human problem solver from a record of selected aspects of his/her problem solving behaviour. The record may be of verbal behaviour (e.g. a 'think-aloud protocol') or of non-verbal behaviour (e.g. eye-movements, or the sequence and timing of moves in a board game). The analysis begins with the building of a **Problem Behaviour Graph** which serves as a 'rational reconstruction' of the solution steps. Regularities are then sought and extracted, possibly in the form of a **production rule system <184>**. Protocol analysis remains an art learned by apprenticeship.

Contributor: Richard Young.

References

Newell, A. On the analysis of human problem solving protocols. In P.C. Johnson-Laird, and P.N. Wason, editors, *Thinking: Readings in Cognitive Science*, pages 46–61. Cambridge University Press, England, 1977.

Ericsson, K.A. and Simon, H.A. Verbal reports as data. *Psychological Review*, 87:215–251, 1980.

192 Pyramids

Alias: **resolution cones**.

Strictly, a pyramid/resolution cone is a set of arrays used to store a digitised image at different resolutions, the highest resolution forming the base of the pyramid. Normally, there is a uniform relationship between adjacent levels of the pyramid, for example, a pixel intensity at a particular resolution is often the average value of the pixel intensities in the corresponding 2 x 2 pixel block at the next highest resolution. More generally, the concept of a regular hierarchical data structure has been extended to include processing elements within the structure, then known as a **processing cone**. Originally, pyramids were used to explicate the relationship between the different image resolutions in a computer vision system using planning. For instance, the boundaries found at a low resolution might be used to refine the **edge detection<71>/ boundary detection <22>** process at higher resolutions. This can significantly improve the efficiency of the overall edge detection process. More recently, it has been realised that image boundaries occur over a wide range of scales from sharp step-like edges to fuzzy, blurred edges. Some results have been stated on using the relationships between corresponding edges occurring at different resolutions to make assertions about the scene boundary producing them. Since these regular hierarchical structures are inappropriate for non-spatial symbolic computation their use is normally restricted to the early processing stage of a vision system.

Contributor: Bob Beattie.

Reference

Tanimoto, S.L.· Regular hierarchical image and processing structures in machine vision. In A.H. Hanson and E.M. Riseman, editors, *Computer Vision Systems.* Academic Press, New York, 1978.

193 Quad Trees

A hierarchical image representation similar to **pyramids** <**192**>, they have nodes that correspond to the cells of a pyramid and each non-terminal node has four children, but unlike a pyramid, a quad tree may be pruned so as to be unbalanced. For example, when all nodes in a subtree have the same gray value, the subtree may be represented by its root without loss of information, so that significant storage savings can be obtained for many images. More significantly, quad trees allow some operations to be performed efficiently by recursive procedures.

Contributor: Luis Jenkins.

Reference

Cohen, P.R. and Feigenbaum, E.A. (editors). *The Handbook of Artificial Intelligence*, Volume 3. Pitman, London, 1982.

194 Qualified Binary Relationship Model

The **QBRM** provides a uniform, efficient, evolvable and expressive framework for knowledge representation. It is based on a **semantic network** <**213**> of

2-place **relations <210>**, in addition to which every relation has two mappings: one onto a set of unique labels (godelisations) and the other onto a set of true-values (true, false, undefined, probable, etc.). This allows every wff to be qualified. The QRBM is formalised in an extended first-order language; it may be used with many-sorted logics. The QRBM is able to support **modal** operators **<142>** and gives a framework for intensional evaluation. The QRBM proving system is a modification to the linear input method, with set-based resolution. QRBM simulators have been written in PASCAL/UNIX and in C/UNIX, using the notion of associatively-accessed quintuples for the low-level storage.

Contributor: Y. J. Jiang and Simon Lavington

Reference

Jiang, Y.J. and Lavington, S.H. The qualified binary relationship model of information. In *Proceedings Conference of Databases No. 4*, pages 61–79, 1985.

195 Qualitative Reasoning

Qualitative Reasoning involves techniques for reasoning with qualitative, rather than numerical values over time. The simplest systems just use the values 'negative', 'zero' and 'positive' and, given a set of qualitative relations, predict all possible qualitative behaviours. It should be contrasted with **naive physics <149>**, which seeks to model human reasoning about the physical world. More complicated systems, like those using **envisioning**, predict the qualitative behaviour of devices, and provide a theory of casuality that can be used to produce causal explanations acceptable to humans.

Qualitative reasoning applies to many areas where exact numerical reasoning is inappropriate or impossible. These include the diagnosis, control, design and explanation of physical or biological systems.

Contributors: Alison Cawsey and Kevin Poulter.

References

Bobrow, D. (editor). *Qualitative Reasoning about Physical Systems.* North Holland, Amsterdam and Oxford, 1984.

de Kleer, J. and Brown, J.S. Foundations of envisioning. In *Proceedings of the AAAI*, pages 434–437. American Association of Artificial Intelligence, 1982.

196 Range Finding

There are several methods for obtaining image depth information by range finding. In **light striping** (a form of **Structured Lighting <231>**), a single plane of light is projected onto a scene. An imaging system is used to detect this reflected light. If the equation of the light plane and the parameters of the imaging system are known then the position in 3D space of each point along the line can be determined. A **spot range** can be determined by emitting a short burst of light (usually with a laser) and measuring the "**time of flight**" of the reflected pulse. An alternative approach is to modulate the light and obtain an estimate of the range from the **phase change** in the returned signal. Instead of light, **ultrasound** can also be used. Range estimates are normally achieved by "time of flight" but ultrasound has the advantage that, unlike light, it is only partially reflected from boundaries enabling range information to be determined through a column of material.

Contributor: H.W. Hughes

Reference

Ballard, D.H. and Brown, C.M. *Computer Vision*, pages 52–56. Prentice-Hall, Englewood Cliffs, London, 1982.

197 Recursion

Recursion theory has been developed by logicians (mainly K. Godel and S.C. Kleene) in the 1930's as a way to formalise metamathematics. Recursive functions can be given by definitions involving reference to the function being defined. For instance

$$f(n) \quad = \quad \text{if} \quad n = 0 \quad \text{then } 1 \text{ else } n * f(n-1)$$

where n is a natural number, is the recursive definition of the factorial.

Since recursive functions are all and only the functions computable by idealised computers (Turing machines), recursion theory has been extended to domains different from the natural numbers (e.g. lists) and used by computer scientists as a powerful tool to reason about programs. Applications include the theory of computation, complexity of programs, program synthesis and program verification.

Contributor: Fausto Giunchiglia.

References

Peter, R. *Recursive Functions in Computer Theory.* Elis Horwood, Chichester, New York, 1981.

Kleene, S. *Introduction to Metamathematics.* Van Nostrand, New York, 1952.

198 Reflectance Map

A reflectance map relates image intensities to surface orientation for given reflectance function, viewpoint and illumination direction. It is usually possible to construct a reflectance map for a surface even under complicated illumination conditions though it may be necessary to measure the intensities empirically as the relation is frequently too complex to be modelled analytically. See also **intrinsic images <113>**.

Contributors: T P Pridmore, S R Pollard, S P Stenton.

Reference

Horn, B.K.P. Understanding image intensities. *Artificial Intelligence*, 8:201–231, 1977.

199 Refutation Proof

Alias: **proof by contradiction, reductio ad absurdum.**

A method of **proof** in which the conjecture is negated and a contradiction deduced thus proving the conjecture to be true. This is the method of proof utilised by most **resolution <204>** theorem provers.

Contributor: Dave Plummer.

Reference

Nilsson, N.J. *Principles of Artificial Intelligence.* Tioga Pub. Co., San Mateo, California, 1980.

200 Region Finding

Alias: **region growing.**

The basic idea of region finding is to produce a **segmentation** of the image in which the regions (connected sets of pixels) found have a useful correspondence to projections of scene entities such as objects or surfaces. As such it is the (currently unpopular) dual of **edge detection <71>/boundary detection <22>**. There are two main approaches:

- Start with the maximum number of regions (eg make every pixel a region) and merge adjacent regions based on some measure of similarity until a satisfactory **segmentation** has been achieved.
- Start with a few (possibly one) large regions and recursively split them into smaller regions based on some measure of dissimilarity until a satisfactory segmentation has been achieved.

Measures of similarity/dissimilarity have ranged from simple average intensities to complex methods incorporating semantics.

Contributor: Bob Beattie.

References

Ballard, D.H. and Brown, C.M. *Computer Vision.* Prentice-Hall, Englewood Cliffs, London, 1982.

Zucker, S.W. Region growing: childhood and adolescence. *Computer Graphics and Image Processing*, 5:382–399, 1976.

201 Regularisation

A method, for determining a solution to an ill-posed mathematical problem, by constraining the solution to be, in some sense, regular or smooth. An ill-posed problem is one for which there does not exist a unique stable solution. The best known regularisation method is that of minimising (with respect to the solution sought) a functional which consists of two terms, the first representing the fidelity of the solution to the data, and the second its smoothness using a constraint measure chosen from physical considerations of the original problem.

Contributor: R.M.Cameron-Jones

Reference

Poggio, T., Torre, V. and Koch, C. Computational Vision and Regularisation Theory *Nature*, 317:314–319, 1985.

202 Relational Database Query Formulation

A technique for specifying queries and other interactions against the Relational and Entity-Relationship Data Models. Database semantics are initially presented as a hierarchy of Functional Areas, leading to Entity-Relationship/Relational description. A naive-user mode provides system initiated dialogue with natural language statements of queries (i.e. paraphrases of Relational Calculus expressions) displayed for user validation. Self-teaching system, with simple 'user controlled' inferencing.

Contributor: Jim Longstaff.

Reference

Longstaff, J. Controlled inference and instruction techniques for DBMS-query languages. In *P111 Proceedings of 1982 ACM SIGMOD Conference*, Association for Computing Machinery, 1982.

203 Relaxation Labelling

Relaxation labelling is a technique for assigning globally consistent labels or values to nodes in a network subject to local constraints, by iteratively propagating the effects of **constraints <43>** through the net. It has its mathematical origins as a technique in numerical analysis for the solution of difference equations and recent developments have shown it to be related to various optimisation techniques eg, linear programming. The first significant application of relaxation labelling to a vision problem was Waltz's **filtering algorithm** in the blocks world **line labelling** domain. Consider the problem of assigning labels to objects to satisfy certain consistency requirements. Unlike a tree representation where each context is explicitly a path, the space may be represented as a graph in which each node carries a set of possible labels. The task is to find a single labelling for each node that satisfies the set of constraints. In general, after an initialisation stage in which each node has been assigned a list of labels and their associated **confidence measures**, the labels and confidences of neighbouring nodes are compared and, guided by the requirement to minimise local inconsistency (often a smoothness constraint), labels are deleted or their confidences adjusted. This process of comparison and adjustment iterates until it converges to some criterion of global consistency. Because both the assignment and updating processes can be done independently at each node, the computation is inherently parallel.

Apart from Waltz's classical application, relaxation labelling has been used in the computation of **optical flow <162>**, the recovery of surface orientation from **shading information <217>**, and the recovery of the orientation structure of images, **stereopsis <227>** and **structure from motion <232>**. The convergence properties of some relaxation operators are not always transparent. The most successful and scientifically useful applications have been when the theoretical analysis of a vision problem reveals a mathematical structure that can be directly exploited in the design of the relaxation algorithm rather than when a 'general operator' has been fitted in an ad hoc fashion to a vision labelling task. See also propagation in **cellular arrays** <**31**>.

Contributor: Jon Mayhew.

References

Davis, L.S. and Rosenfeld, A. Cooperating processes in low level. *Artificial Intelligence*, 17:246–265, 1981.

Ballard, D.H. and Brown, C.M. *Computer Vision.* Prentice-Hall, Englewood Cliffs, London, 1982.

204 Resolution

A **rule of inference** of **predicate calculus** <**180**> used to deduce a new formula from two old ones. It has been used extensively in **automatic theorem proving**, because it is an efficient alternative to traditional rules of inference in mathematical logic. All the three formulae involved must be in **clausal form** <**36**>. If C and D are **clauses** and the P_i and Q_j are atomic formulae then the rule is

$$\frac{C \vee P_1 \vee \ldots \vee P_m \qquad D \vee \sim Q_1 \vee \ldots \vee \sim Q_m}{(C \vee D)\theta}$$

where θ is the most general **unifier** of all the P_i and Q_j, and is obtained by **unification** <**248**>. Resolution is the execution mechanism of **Prolog** <**187**>.

Contributor: Alan Bundy.

Reference

Chang, C. and Lee, R.C. *Symbolic Logic and Mechanical Theorem Proving.* Academic Press, New York, 1973.

205 Rewrite Rules

Alias: **condition-action pairs, demodulants.**

Rewrite rules are sets of ordered pairs of expressions (lhs,rhs) usually depicted as (lhs => rhs). There is usually a similarity relation between the 'lhs' and the 'rhs' such as equality, inequality or double implication. Rewrite rules, as the pairs are called, together with the rewriting **rule of inference** allow one expression to be 'rewritten' into another. A subexpression of the initial expression is matched with the 'lhs' of the rewrite rule yielding a **substitution**. The resulting expression is the expression obtained by replacing the distinguished subexpression with the 'rhs' of the rewrite rule after applying the substitution.

The matching process may be full **unification** <**248**> or, more usually, a restricted form of **Pattern Matching** <**169**> where only the variables in the rewrite rule may be instantiated. Examples of the use of rewrite rules are the restricted paramodulation <**164**> inferences called demodulation performed in theorem provers or programming with abstract data types introduced by a series of equations. Some powerful theoretical results have been obtained for rewriting systems.

Contributor: Lincoln Wallen.

Reference

Huet, G. and Oppen, D.C. *Equations and Rewrite Rules: A Survey.* Technical Report CSL-111, SRI International, January 1980.

206 Robot Dynamics

Robot dynamics addresses the problems of calculating the acceleration of a robot from a given set of forces (forward dynamics), and calculating the forces required to produce a given acceleration (inverse dynamics). Forward dynamics is used for **simulation**, inverse dynamics for control. A robot is considered to be a system of rigid bodies, or links, connected together by joints. The laws of motion for rigid bodies are used to find the equations of motion for the robot. The two main approaches are via Newton's and Euler's equations, and via Lagrange's equation. The tricky part is to calculate the answers efficiently. This is done by expressing the equations of motion in terms of recurrence relations between the motion of one link and that of one of its neighbours in such a way that the answers may be calculated recursively.

Contributor: Roy Featherstone.

References

Hollerbach, J.M. A recursive lagrangian formulation of manipulator dynamics and a comparative study of dynamics formulation complexity. *IEEE Trans. Systems, Man & Cybernetics*, SMC-10(11):730–736, 1980.

Walker, M.W. and Orin, D.E. Efficient dynamic computer simulation of robotic mechanisms. *Trans. ASME, ser. G, Jnl. Dyn. Sys. Measurement & Control*, 104:205–211, 1982.

Paul, R.P. *Robot manipulators.* MIT Press, Cambridge, Mass., 1981.

207 Robot Programming

The principle advantage of the industrial robot over conventional automation is programmability. The robot extends the capabilities of **NC machine tools <156>** by performing motions necessary for transferring parts and tools, forging, casting, painting, assembly, welding, and so forth. More flexible machining operations can also be performed by robots, but at the cost of precision. The requirements of robot programming systems are in specifying motions, controlling devices, flow of control, world modelling, and specifying the use of sensors. Four levels of abstraction in robot programming can be identified: (1) actuator level, in which axis values (joint angles) are specified for each step of the task; (2) end-effector level, in which the position of the tool is specified in any of several coordinate systems such as **cartesian coordinates** and Euler angles; (3) object level, in which the task is described in terms of operations on objects ('insert pin in hole'); and (4) objective level, in which the user specifies the task in a declarative form, and is not required to specify the manner in which the task is performed. All industrial robots permit level 1 operations, and many robots have level 2 capabilities. Level 3 is currently represented by laboratory systems such as **RAPT** and **AUTOPASS**. Level 4 is the subject of research:

automatic planners and declarative languages such as **Prolog <187>** may be expected to contribute to this area.

Contributor: W.F. Clocksin.

References

Koutsou, A. *A survey of model-based robot programming languages.* Working Paper 108, Dept. of Artificial Intelligence, Edinburgh, 1981.

Lozano-Perez, T. *Robot programming.* Memo 698, MIT AI Lab, 1982.

208 Scale-Space Representation

The representation of an image quantity (*e.g.* zero-crossings) over a range (which may in theory vary continuously) of scales at which the image is perceived. The "scale" concerned is generally the width parameter of a Gaussian function with which the image is convolved; thus at small scales the image detail is faithfully represented and at large scales the detail is blurred as the result tends to the image mean.

Contributor: R.M. Cameron-Jones

Reference

Witkin, A.P. Scale-space filtering, *Proceedings of IJCAI-83*, pages 1019–1022. International Joint Conference on Artificial Intelligence, 1983.

209 Script

A structure for the large scale organisation of knowledge, adopted by Schank primarily as a support for natural language understanding, and related to **conceptual dependency <38>** as the primary form of knowledge representation. Scripts define the normal character and sequence of events in, for example, a restaurant visit as a temporal incident. They can thus be used to assign an order to language data that do not give temporal information explicitly, and may also be used to indicate underlying causal relationships. The need for explicit inference to determine temporal or causal relations between data instances is therefore reduced. In Schank's view the event orientation of scripts distinguishes them from other **frames** <**84**>, but they share other properties of frames, e.g. defaults and attached procedures, and forms of set organisation, and present similar problems of definition and use. Scripts have been applied to a wide variety of language processing tasks (e.g. **MOPS**), chiefly by the Yale group. In general, usage of the term is less variable than that of frame, but it is still applied with a good deal of freedom.

Contributor: Karen Sparck Jones.

Reference

Schank, R. and Abelson, R. *Scripts, Plans, Goals and Understanding.* Lawrence Erlbaum Associates, Hillsdale, New Jersey, 1977.

210 Semantic Binary Relationship Model

This is an information model suitable for a smart database, and also for knowledge representation when large amounts of data are expected. The SBRM is a **semantic net** <**213**> formed by providing a **Binary Relationship model** with several built-in entities and relationships with pre-defined semantics. These give the structural and abstraction mechanisms for classifying data and for the generalisation/specialisation of classes into hierarchies. The resulting class structure proves useful for implementing several aspects of **integrity checking**, **concurrency control**, inheritance rules and **inference**. Since the n-place predicates of logic are represented in the semantic network by (n+1) binary relationships (i.e. 2-place predicates), explicit rules may be represented in the SBRM. A version of the SBRM has been implemented in C/Unix, using the notion of associatively-accessed triples for the low-level storage.

Contributors: M. Azmoodeh and Simon Lavington.

References

Azmoodeh, M., Lavington, S.H. and Standring, M. The semantic binary relation model of information. Department of Computer Science, University of Essex, 1984.

Azmoodeh. M. and Dunnion, J.N. *A BRM machine and its interface procedures.* Internal Report IFS/4/84, Dept. of Computer Science, University of Manchester, 1984.

211 Semantic Checking

Alias: **use of models.**

A technique for pruning a **search space** of a logical inference mechanism, e.g. **resolution** <**204**> or **natural deduction** <**150**>. One or more models are given of the axioms and hypotheses of a problem. If the model is not a counterexample then the goal is also true in the model(s). All subgoals false in any model are pruned from the search space. This technique preserves completeness if the problem consists only of **Horn clauses** <**36**>.

Contributor: Alan Bundy.

Reference

Gelernter, H. *Realisation of a Geometry theorem-proving machine.* McGraw-Hill, New York, 1963.

212 Semantic Grammar

Semantic grammar is contrasted with conventional grammars as it relies predominantly on semantic rather than syntactic categories, e.g.

MESSAGE $\rightarrow$ PATIENT-TYPE HAVE DISEASE-TYPE

In some cases the semantic categories and structures are merely cosmetic relabellings of conventional syntactic categories and structures, but more thorough semantic grammars are widely used, though even these typically contain some mixture of syntactic elements. Semantic grammars have been found especially effective for language processing in limited domain contexts, e.g. processing medical records, interpreting database queries, where syntactic parsing is unnecessarily costly, but general-purpose semantic grammars have also been proposed. There is a connection between these grammars and **semantic primitives <214>** and semantic **case frames <30>**. However systems making heavy use of general-purpose semantics are not conventionally described as relying on semantic grammars.

Contributor: Karen Sparck Jones.

Reference

Brownm, J.S. and Burton, R. Multiple representations of knowledge for tutorial reasoning. In D.G. Bobrow and A. Collins, editors, *Representation and Understanding*, pages 311–349. Academic Press, New York, 1975.

213 Semantic Net

Alias: **semantic network.**

A principle for the large scale organisation of knowledge emphasising the multiple associations of individual concepts. Concepts, objects, entities, etc. are represented as **nodes** in a **linked** graph, and relationships between these are represented as labeled arcs. The range of possible network structure types is very wide (see Findler). Semantic nets should properly be based on definitions of the net structure, i.e. the syntax and semantics of nodes and links and of configurations of these, and of net operations, i.e. the syntax and semantics of node-node transitions, but too frequently are not. Nets have been found an attractive descriptive device, but genuine algorithmic exploitation of nets based e.g. on the general idea of **Marker-passing <134>** for selective reading or writing at nodes, is comparatively rare (formal graph theory is rarely seriously invoked in artificial intelligence). The emphasis on concept association introduces difficulties in representing any partitioning or grouping of net elements, for example to represent quantified propositions, clusters of similar entities, etc.

(but see **partitioned net <166>**), and network searching conspicuously manifests the general AI problem of the **combinatorial explosion**.

Contributor: Karen Sparck Jones.

Reference

Findler, N.V. (editor). *Associative Networks*, Academic Press, New York, 1979.

214 Semantic Primitives

The general concepts underlying words, used for the determination and representation of textual or propositional meaning, e.g. MOVE underlies 'walk' and 'run', THING 'vase' and 'book'. Semantic primitives are used to define selection criteria for sense identification, and to define key properties e.g. of **case frame <30>** role fillers. Primitives, which should in principle be drawn from a closed set, may be shallow or deep i.e. more or less fine-grained, domain-independent or domain-dependent, categorial or relational, etc. The characterisations of word (senses) may be by single primitives, primitive sets, or structured formulae, and the primitive characterisations of sentences may be more or less elaborately structured. The primitive names may be regarded as elements of a distinct meaning representation language, or as selected elements of the language under description. Though primitives universally figure in some form or other in language understanding systems, they are more frequently adopted ad hoc than systematically motivated. Wilks and Schank are exceptions here.

Contributor: Karen Sparck Jones.

Reference

Charniak, E. and Wilks, Y. *Computational Semantics*. North-Holland, Amsterdam and Oxford, 1976.

215 Sensory Feedback and Compliance

A common problem in robotics is to bring a tool to a certain spatial relationship to a workpiece, or to bring two or more components together into a certain spatial relationship. However, owing to accumulation of dimensional variation and tolerances that cannot be minimised at their source, errors can occur, making it unexpectedly difficult or impossible to solve this problem by dead reckoning. Thus, in many cases, a robot must be able to detect that components are poorly positioned, and it must have the ability to make small incremental changes in position to minimise the error. 'Sensing', or the measurement of physical properties (optical, acoustic, tactile, etc) can be used actively to detect displacements from the correct position; the resulting error signal is fed back to steer the robot in the direction to minimise the error. This is known as closed-loop control, which is formalised by **Control Theory**. Compliance is a passive control technique, where springs and other mechanical devices are used to produce corrective displacements in reaction to forces in the tool.

Contributor: W.F. Clocksin.

References

Simons, G.L. *Robots in Industry.* NCC Publications, 1980.

Nevins, J.L. and Whitney, D.E. Computer controlled assembly. *Scientific American*, 238(2):62–74, February 1978.

Dorf, R.C. *Modern Control Systems.* Addison-Wesley, Reading, Mass. and Wokingham, 1980.

216 Sequent Calculus

A method of presenting a logic invented by Gentzen in which statements are made in the form

$$A_1, A_2, \ldots A_n \Rightarrow B_1, B_2, \ldots B_m$$

where the sequent sign "$\Rightarrow$" indicates that given all the propositions A_i one of the propositions B_j holds. A logic is characterised by giving basic sequents as axioms and then allowing further sequents to be derived using rules of inference, typically associated with the introduction and elimination of the logical symbols of the language on either side of the arrow; for example, one of the rules for introducing a disjunction is,

$$\frac{\Gamma \Rightarrow \Theta, P}{\Gamma \Rightarrow \Theta,\ P \vee Q}$$

where Γ and Θ represent an arbitrary number of propositions. One of the advantages of sequent calculus over, say, **Natural Deduction <150>** is the ease with which proofs can be manipulated (eg Gentzen's work on proof theory).

Contributor: Alan Smaill.

Reference

Gallier, J.H. *Logic for computer science: foundations of automatic theorem proving.* Harper & Row, New York and London, 1986.

217 Shape from Shading

The process of extracting three-dimensional shape information from smooth gradations of reflected light intensity. It has been shown by Horn that if certain assumptions are made concerning the reflectance function and illumination of a surface it is possible to formulate and solve equations relating surface shape to the measured intensities in an image of the surface. See **intrinsic images <113>**.

Contributors: T P Pridmore, S R Pollard, S T Stenton.

Reference

Horn, R.K.P. Obtaining shape from shading information. In P.H. Winston, editor, *The Psychology of Computer Vision.* McGraw-Hill, New York, 1975.

218 Shape from Texture

Shape from texture is the process by which the three-dimensional structure of a surface is determined from the spatial distribution of surface markings. Projection into the image plane distorts the geometry of surface textures in a manner dependent upon the shape of the underlying surface: as a surface recedes from the viewer its markings appear smaller due to perspective effects, and as a surface is inclined away from the frontal plane its markings appear compressed in the direction of the inclination. By isolating these projective distortions it is possible to recover the shape of a textured surface.

Contributors: T. P. Pridmore, S. R. Pollard, S. T. Stenton.

Reference

Witkin, A.P. Recovering surface shape and orientation from texture. *Artificial Intelligence*, 17:17–45, 1981.

219 Simulated Annealing

Simulated Annealing is a technique for solving combinatorial optimisation problems by means of the Metropolis Algorithm. Optimisation requires the use of an objective function (or evaluation function), which represents a quantitative measure of the 'goodness' of a proposed solution. A conventional technique for iterative improvement considers local changes to a proposed solution, accepting just those changes that improve the solution. On realistic problems, this can lead to a local optimum at which all subsequent changes do not improve the solution, even though better solutions are available some distance away.

By contrast, in an annealing system, the acceptance of a proposed change depends on a function of both the goodness of the change and a Gaussian noise source. The standard deviation of the noise begins high and is gradually reduced according to a predetermined 'annealing schedule' until no further changes occur.

The term 'annealing' is suggested by the formal connection between statistical thermodynamics and combinatorial optimisation. Simulated annealing is being applied in perception and learning research, and in computer-aided design.

Contributors: W. F. Clocksin, Geoffrey Sampson.

Reference

Kirkparick, S., Gelatt, C.D. and Vecchi, M.P. Optimisation by simulated annealing. *Science*, 220:671–680, 1983.

220 Situation Calculus

A technique for representing time or different situations in an assertional database. Each relation/property which changes over time is given an extra argument place, which is filled with a situation term. In **plan formation** this situation argument is usually a nested term representing the sequence of plan steps needed to get to this situation from the initial state. Thus situations label the effect of actions and can represent alternative futures, whereas a numerically measured time can only represent a unique future.

Contributor: Alan Bundy.

Reference

Nilsson, N.J. *Principles of Artificial Intelligence.* Tioga Pub. Co., San Mateo, California, 1980.

221 Skeletonisation

This is a transformation of a binary image which locates the central axis ('**skeleton**' or '**medial-axis**') of each object in the image. The general principle is to thin each object in the image to a line structure by repeatedly deleting edge pixels whose demise will not change the connectivity of the image.

Algorithms are available which can also deal with three dimensional binary images.

Contributor: Dave Reynolds.

Reference

Tsao, Y.F. and Fu, K.S. A parallel thinning algorithm for 3-d pictures. *Computer Graphics and Image Processing*, 17:315–331, 1981.

222 Skolemization

A technique borrowed from **mathematical logic** (and named after the mathematician Skolem), but much used in **automatic theorem proving**, for removing **quantifiers** from **predicate calculus** <**180**> formulae. If A(y) is a formula with free variables $y, x_1, \ldots, x_n$, then $\forall y\, A(y)$ is replaced by A(y), and $\exists y\, A(y)$ is replaced by $A(f(x_1,...,x_n))$, where f is a new **Skolem function**. The technique is usually applied to formulae which have all their quantifiers at the front (**Prenex normal form**), but can be adapted to any formula. It produces a formula which has a model if and only if the original formula does. It is one of the techniques used in turning a formulae into **clausal form** <**36**>

Contributor: Alan Bundy.

Reference

Chang, C. and Lee, R.C. *Symbolic Logic and Mechanical Theorem Proving.* Academic Press, New York, 1973.

223 Spatial Frequency Channels

Spatial frequency channels are systems sensitive to a limited range of spatial frequencies. In the human visual system these are considered to be a population of cells with similar tuning characteristics specifically sensitive to a restricted range of the **contrast sensitivity function <48>** envelope. See **bandpass filter <14>**.

Contributors: T P Pridmore, S R Pollard, S T Stenton.

Reference

Wilson, H.R. and Bergen, J.R. A fourier mechanism model for spatial vision. *Vision Research*, 19:19–32, 1979.

224 Spelling Correction

An essential requirement for serious natural language processing programs, though not strictly an AI technique.

A simple strategy, based on a letter-by-letter tree-structured dictionary, assumes that errors fall into the four types: (i) extra letter (ii) substituted letter (iii) omitted letter and (iv) reversed latter pair. Then at any point where a mismatch between input string and dictionary string occurs a new match can be tried by, respectively, (i) advancing the input string one letter (ii) advancing both strings together (iii) advancing the dictionary string, and (iv) advancing first one string and then the other.

This strategy is looking for letter position correspondence between the two strings; weaker strategies look merely for ordinal correspondence, and yet weaker for 'material' correspondence, i.e. just having the same letters. The simple strategy described does not take account of the number of errors per word. Generalising for this requires a string similarity measure. Such measures allow the use of non-literal word representations, e.g. hash coding, and of n-gram rather than single-letter based matching. Spelling correction may also use heuristics exploiting e.g. distinctive properties of the language ('u' after 'q' in English), those of the input device (optical character reader, human typist), and the choice of strategy may be influenced by the task e.g. whether a large lexicon is involved, whether a user should be consulted for a proposed correction, etc. In the limit, error detection and correction requires full language understanding.

Contributor: Karen Sparck Jones.

Reference

Pollock, J.J. Spelling error detection and correction by computer: some notes and a bibliography. *Journal of Documentation*, 38:282–291, 1982.

225 Standard ML

A **functional language** <87> where functions are first-class data objects (ie it is higher order); the language is interactive and statically scoped <**246**>. Standard ML is strongly **typed** <**246**> with a polymorphic type system. Abstract data types are supported, together with a type-safe exception mechanism. Standard ML also has a modules facility to support the incremental construction of large programs.

Contributor: Kevin Mitchell

References

Harper, R., MacQueen, D. and Milner, R. *Standard ML.* LFCS Report ECS-LFCS-86-2, Department of Computer Science, Edinburgh University, Scotland.

A. Wikström. *Functional Programming Using Standard ML.* Prentice Hall, Hemel hemstead, 1987.

226 State Space

Alias: **search space, problem space.**

Many problems can be represented as an initial state, a goal state and a set of **operators** <159> that define operations to go to new states from a given state. The states that can be reached from the initial state by applying the rules in all possible ways define the state space. The problem is then to reach the goal state from the initial state. By this formulation almost any problem can be reduced to a search problem.

Contributor: Maarten van Someren.

Reference

Barr, A. and Feigenbaum, E.A. (editors). *The Handbook of Artificial Intelligence*, Volume 1. W. Kaufmann, Los Altos, California, 1981.

227 Stereopsis

The process of recovering the 3D structure of a scene from two different views. The problem has two parts; the measurement of the disparity of corresponding points in the two images, and the interpretation of these disparity measurements to recover the range and orientation of the surfaces in the scene. See **intrinsic images <113>** and **relaxation labelling <113>**.

Contributors: T P Pridmore, S R Pollard, S R Stenton.

Reference

Mayhew, J.E.W. Stereopsis. In Braddick and Sleigh, editors, *Physical and Biological Processing of Images*, 1983.

228 Stochastic Geometry

The representation of parameters associated with geometric primitives as stochastic processes; thus enabling the application of techniques from stochastic filtering theory. It is most commonly used in problems of data fusion, where the (possibly Extended) **Kalman Filter** is the best known tool as in most application areas of stochastic filtering.

Contributor: R.M. Cameron-Jones

Reference

Ayache, N. and Faugeras, O.D. Building, registrating and fusing noisy visual maps. *International Journal of Robotics Research*, 7(6):pp45–65, 1988.

229 Stochastic Simulation

Alias: **Gibbs Sampling.**

A method of computing probabilities by counting how frequently events occur in a series of simulation runs. In each run the occurrence of an event is determined by sampling a random distribution, reflecting the current state of related events as well as the strength of interaction among them. In **Boltzman machines** stochastic simulation is used together with **annealing** <219> to find the state of lowest energy.

Contributor: Judea Pearl.

Reference

Pearl, J. *Probabilistic Reasoning in Intelligent Systems: networks of plausible inference.* Morgan Kaufmann, San Mateo, California, 1988.

230 Structured Induction

Structured induction employs the same top-down problem decomposition as structured programming, combined with bottom-up implementation of the individual subproblems. A given problem is split into relevant attributes, those attributes that are not directly codable are split again. This decomposition process is repeated for each attribute that is not immediately codable until none is left, producing a hierarchical tree of subproblems whose leaf nodes are directly codable attributes. Inductive inference is then used to solve each of the subproblems from the bottom of this hierarchy to the top. Each newly solved subproblem is given a meaningful name which is used in the next level up as a simple coded attribute. This process is continued until there are no more subproblem hierarchy levels to ascend. A top level procedure now exists that when run, calls the lower level subproblems and attributes in an order determined by the inductive procedures applied at each level of the bottom-up implementation. This technique was developed at the Machine Intelligence Research Unit, University of Edinburgh as an aid to the generation of humanly understandable classification rules for use in expert systems.

Contributor: Alen Shapiro.

Reference

Shapiro, A. and Niblett, R.B. Automatic induction of classification rules for a chess end-game. In *Advances in Computer Chess, 3*, Pergamon Press, Oxford, 1982.

231 Structured Light

The use of the geometry of the illumination actively emitted into the scene to simplify the task of inferring environmental structure. It is often used for **Range Finding <196>**. The best known example of structed ligh is illuminating the scene with a (scanning) light-stripe enabling the direct interpretation of breaks in the sensed line as depth discontinuities in the scene. With knowledge of the geometric position of the light source and the relative position of the sensor system, the scene position of the observed stripe can often be calculated.

Contributor: R.M. Cameron-Jones

Reference

Popplestone, R.J., Brown, C.M., Ambler, A. P. and Crawford, G. F., Forming models of plane-and-cylinder faceted bodies from light stripes. *Proceedings of IJCAI-75*, pp 664–668, International Joint Conference on Artificial Intelligence, 1975.

232 Structure from Motion

The calculation of three-dimensional global structure from the two-dimensional properties of features visible in a time series of images. The features are usually points, but may be lines, etc. Most methods require the correspondence of features between images and rely upon the **rigidity assumption** - the assumption that the environment is rigid. There are many results on the number of views required for a minimal solution to exist for a given number of points visible in all the images, amongst which the best known (first derived for orthographic projection by Ullman under the rigidity assumption) is that three views of four points are required. In a rigid environment, the method is a form of stereo - the determination of structure from images taken from more than one viewpoint.

Contributor: R.M. Cameron-Jones

Reference

Faugeras, O. D., Lustman, F. and Toscani, G. Motion and structure from motion from point and line matches *Proceedings of the First International Conference on Computer Vision*, pp25-34, 1987.

233 Subgoaling

Alias: **problem reduction.**

Many planning systems use a **backwards search** of the space that is defined by the available **operators <159>**. The goal is split into subgoals, and the system then recursively tries to satisfy those subgoals. A major problem with this method is that the subgoals may be interdependent. To achieve subgoal G1 it may be necessary to apply an operator that makes it impossible to achieve subgoal G2. See **Interactions Between Sub-goals <111>**.

Contributor: Maarten van Someren.

References

Nilsson, N.J. *Principles of Artificial Intelligence*, Tioga Pub. Co., Palo Alto, California, 1980.

Stefik, M.J. Planning with constraints (Molgen: part 1) and planning and meta-planning (Molgen: part2). *Artificial Intelligence*, 16:111–139 and 16:141–169, 1981.

Sussman, G.J. *A computer model of skill acquisition.* Elsevier, New York, 1975.

234 Superquadrics

Superquadrics are a set of parameterised volumetric shapes used for computer vision applications. They are useful because a wide range of solid shapes can be generated by use of only a few parameters. Surface patches can be defined by the surface of a superquadric volume. Additionally, more complex objects can be defined by combinations of simpler volumes using union, intersection and complement.

Any superquadric may be expressed by the equation

$$\chi(\eta,\omega) = \begin{pmatrix} a1cos^{\varepsilon1}\eta cos^{\varepsilon2}\omega \\ a2cos^{\varepsilon1}\eta sin^{\varepsilon2}\omega \\ a3sin^{\varepsilon1}\eta \end{pmatrix}$$

where $-\pi/2 \leq \eta \leq \pi/2$ and $-\pi \leq \omega < \pi$, $a1$, $a2$ and $a3$ are the length, width and breadth respectively. $\varepsilon1$ and $\varepsilon2$ are the parameters which specify the shape of the superquadric. $\varepsilon1$ is the squareness parameter in the north-south direction. $\varepsilon2$ is the squareness parameter in the east-west direction. The advantage of this representation is that the normal vectors are given by

$$n(\eta,\omega) = \begin{pmatrix} \frac{1}{a1}cos^{2-\varepsilon1}\eta cos^{2-\varepsilon2}\omega \\ \frac{1}{a2}cos^{2-\varepsilon1}\eta sin^{2-\varepsilon2}\omega \\ \frac{1}{a3}sin^{2-\varepsilon1}\eta \end{pmatrix}$$

enabling the shape parameters to be recovered via surface normal information from image intensity, contour shape and the like.

These mathematical solids are a subset of the more general family of **Generalised Cylinders <90>**.

Contributor: H.W. Hughes

Reference

Barr, A.H. Superquadrics and angle-preserving transformations. *IEEE Computer Graphics and Applications*, 1:1–20.

235 Surface Reconstruction

Recovering object surface information can be achieved in a number of ways. **Stereopsis <227>** will yield explicit surface information only at those points where a direct correspondence is achievable. Analysis of motion or **optical flow <162>** also yields surface information but again the data is sparse. By using a "thin plate" and deforming it to fit the available constraints it is possible to obtain an *approximation* to the object surface. By varying the resolution to which the thin plate is deformed it is possible to form a hierarchy of surface descriptions. At the lowest level these include texture descriptions while at higher levels coarser shape information is represented.

Contributor: H.W. Hughes

Reference

Terzopoulos, D. Multilevel computational processes for visual surface reconstruction. *Computer Vision, Graphics and Image Processing*, 24:52–96, 1983.

236 Surface Segmentation

A form of **region finding <200>** that organises data from a range image into patches with a coherent property, usually based on some form of local surface shape. The two principal curvatures **principal curvature** or the mean and Gaussian curvatures are often used for purely data-driven segmentation; that is, all adjacent image pixels with similar curvatures are grouped to form a patch. Refinements include using only the signs of the curvatures to produce larger patches and to overcome noise, and prohibiting merging across depth discontinuities. Another refinement fits quadratic (or higher order) surfaces to stable patches and then incrementally grows the regions by adding image pixels that lie close to the estimated surface.

Contributor: Robert B. Fisher

Reference

Besl, P. *Surfaces in Range Image Understanding.* Springer-Verlag, New York and London, 1988.

237 Symbolic Marker-passing

Alias: **Non-numeric spreading activation, Von Neumann Machine Connectionism**

Based on early work by Quillian (1966), symbolic marker-passing is used an efficient search which finds paths through a **semantic net <213>**. This search is usually characterised by being **breadth-first <26>**, massively parallelisable, and non-deductive. The canonical example of the need for marker-passing is found in the story "John wanted to commit suicide. He picked up a rope." To find that the context of the story is "hang" requires the spread of information through the network, and the finding of the path: SUICIDE, KILL, HANG, NOOSE, ROPE. This formulation of marker-passing has been applied in natural language processing and planning research. Recent research has been examining integrating this technique with that of **local connectionism**. See also **Marker-passing <134>**.

Contributor: James A.Hendler

Reference

Charniak, E. Passing markers: a theory of contextual influence in language comprehension. *Cognitive Science*, 7:171–190, 1983.

238 Table of Multiple Effects

This is a table (first used in the **NOAH** planner) relating patterns (representing facts) to nodes in a plan where they are asserted or denied. It is used by **non-linear planners <154>** to detect quickly interferences between actions on parallel branches. However, it can also be used to recognise beneficial **side effects** which may allow other goals to be satisfied without introducing new actions.

Contributor: Austin Tate.

Reference

Sacerdoti, E.D. *A Structure for plans and behaviour.* Elsevier North-Holland, New York, 1977.

239 Template Matching

A simple technique that is sometimes used in language understanding. A language unit (sentence or phrase) is compared with a set of predefined 'templates'. Some positions in the template consist of variables that match any input. If a template matches the input, the variables take the value of the corresponding elements in the input. Eg. the template 'Var1 hits Var2' matches the input 'Mary hits John with her hand' and Var1 takes the value 'Mary' and Var2 'John with her hand'. Template matching is only useful if there is a small number of templates, otherwise the matching process is too expensive.

Contributor: Maarten van Someren.

Reference

Barr, A. and Feigenbaum, E.A. (editors). *The Handbook of Artificial Intelligence*, Volume 1. W. Kaufmann, Los Altos, California, 1981.

240 Temporal Logic

Temporal logic deals with reasoning about time. There are three different approaches to temporal logic. The first approach is the **Situation Calculus <220>**. In the situation calculus, one simply adds an argument to each predicate which represents the time at which the predicate is assumed to be true. Thus, a two-place predicate like "hit" becomes a three-place predicate, and the proposition that Harry loves Mary at time t is represented simply as "hit(harry,mary,t)". The second approach is the reified approach. In the reified approach, of which the **Event Calculus** is an example, one complicates the language by introducing separate terms for events, processes etc. as well as a predicate which is sometimes called `HOLDS`, sometimes `TT`, for saying that an event took place at some time. So, to express the proposition that Harry hit Mary at time t, one would write `HOLDS(hit(harry,mary),t)`, where `hit(harry,mary)` is a functional expression denoting the event of Harry hitting Mary. The final and third approach, which has has not been too popular in AI, is **modal temporal logic**. One introduces a number of **modal** operators **<142>**, such as `P` (for past) and `F` (for future) and uses these to represent time-dependent information. For example, the information that Harry hit Mary in the past is represented as `P(hit(harry,mary))`.

Reasoning about time is important in a number of areas in AI. In planning for example you have to reason about the effects that an action will have on the world, and this involves reasoning about future states of affairs. Another example is natural language processing where one is concerned with extracting temporal information from the tenses of sentences.

Contributor: Han Reichgelt.

References

Galton, A. *Temporal Logics and their applications.* Academic Press, London, 1987.

Turner, R. *Logics for Artificial Intelligence.* Wiley, New York, 1984.

241 Theorem Proving

Alias: **automatic theorem proving, mechanical theorem proving, computational logic.**

The goal of theorem proving is to use mechanical methods for finding proofs of theorems to perform automated reasoning. The implementation language is usually **first order logic <180>**, or some other sound and complete formalism. The problem can be stated as follows: given a set of hypotheses (axioms and/or theorems), a set of rules (called the rules of inference) which allow new facts to be derived from old, a given formula (the goal) should be derived in finitely many applications of the rules of inference.

Besides mathematical reasoning, which is the obvious application, many problems can be transformed into theorem proving problems: question-answering systems, program-synthesis, program verification, state transformation problems and so on.

Some theorem proving techniques are based on Herbrand's theorem (eg **resolution <204>**, **connection method <39>**) but some attempts have been made using **natural deduction** based, and induction based systems **<23>**. The reference provides a very good collection of many of the early attempts (up to 1970) in theorem proving.

Contributor: Fausto Giunchiglia.

Reference

Siekmann, J. and Wrightson, G. (editors). *Automation of Reasoning.* Springer-Verlag, Berlin, 1983. Published in 2 volumes.

242 Time Logic Based Planning

Propositions, and actions and their component sub-actions, may be related to the time intervals over which the respectively hold and occur. This enables a substantial part of the planning process to be undertaken by a general temporal reasoner utilising a suitable **Temporal Logic <240>**. The combinatorial cost, however, may be high.

Contributor: Jim Doran

References

Allen, J.F. and Koomen, J.A. Planning using a temporal world model. In *Proceedings of IJCAI-83*, pages 741 – 747, International Joint Conference on Artificial Intelligence, 1983.

Tsang, P.K. Plan generation in a temporal frame. In *Proceedings ECAI-86*, pages 479 – 493, European Conference on Artificial Intelligence, 1986.

243 Top-down Parsing

Alias: **hypothesis-driven parsing.**

In trying to parse a string with a grammar, if one starts with the grammar and tries to fit it to the string, this is top-down parsing. For instance with a **context-free grammar <45>**, one starts with expansions for the initial symbol, and builds down from there trying to find an expansion which will get to the symbols in the string.

Contributor: Henry Thompson.

Reference

Winograd, T. *Language as a cognitive process.* Addison-Wesley, Reading, Mass. and London, 1983.

244 Trinocular Stereo

A method for calculating a (generally sparse) depth map for a scene by corresponding (features of) three intensity images taken from different viewpoints.

The major advantages of using three images rather than two (as used in biologically motivated binocular stereo) are the rejection of many of the false correspondences which may arise in the two image case and the improvement in the accuracy of the estimated depth as a consequence of using the extra data.

Contributor: R.M. Cameron-Jones

Reference

Ayache, N. and Lustman, F. Fast and reliable passive trinocular stereovision. *First International Conference on Computer Vision*, pages 422–427, 1987.

245 Truth Maintenance System

Alias: **reason maintenance system.**

A truth maintenance system (TMS) is used to record justifications for assertions. Such justifications can be used to generate explanations and to track down the assumptions underlying assertions. For example, in **RUP** every justification is a disjunctive clause of sentential (propositional) atoms and any such clause can be treated as a justification. RUP's TMS takes a set of such propositional clauses and performs propositional **constraint propagation <43>** to ensure that every assertion with a valid justification is in fact believed by the system (thus ensuring a deduction **invariant**). RUP's TMS also ensures that there is an entry on a contradiction queue for every propositional clause all of whose atoms are false.

Contributor: D. McAllester.

References

Doyle, J. *Truth Maintenance Systems for Problem Solving.* Technical Report 419, MIT AI Lab, Cambridge, Mass., September 1978.

McAllester, D. *An Outlook on Truth Maintenance.* Technical Report 551, MIT AI Lab, Cambridge, Mass., August 1980.

246 Typed Languages

In a typed language, every value is partitioned into one or more sets called types. Every legal expression denotes a value, and hence has a type. Some languages require typing information to be supplied explicitly, and the types of subexpressions in an expression are then checked for consistency by a type checker. Other languages make use of a type inference system to determine this information. Programming languages in which the type of every expression can be determined by static program analysis are said to be statically scoped. Languages in which all expressions are type consistent are called **strongly typed languages**. Strong typing guarantees that no program can incur a type error at run time, a common source of bugs. **Standard ML <225>** is an example of a strongly typed language.

Contributor: Kevin Mitchell

Reference

Cardelli, L. and Wegner, P. On understanding types, data abstraction, and polymorphism. *Computing Surveys*, 17(4):471–522, 1985.

247 Typed Preconditions

In early problem solving systems (eg **STRIPS**) and planning languages (eg **PLANNER**) the operators were given a single set of preconditions which were always interpreted as 'test if true, or subgoal to make them true'. The need to distinguish between the case in which the planner should only check if something was already true or should be allowed to add further actions into a plan to make the condition true was recognised as an important search control mechanism in **POPLER**. This led to two different types of precondition. Additions were also made to various pattern directed invocation systems which clustered alternative methods together and made a choice from them on the basis of some pre-occurring fact.

The utility of typed preconditions and their different properties for both hierarchic domain description and planner search space control was investigated in the **NONLIN** <154> planner which recognised 4 precondition types: SUPERVISED, UNSUPERVISED, USEWHEN and ACHIEVE.

Contributor: Austin Tate.

References

Davies, D.J.M. *POPLER l.5 Reference Manual.* Technical Report, Department of Aritificial Intelligence, Edinburgh University, 1973.

Tate, A. Generating project networks. In *Proceedings IJCAI-77*, pages 888–893. International Joint Conference on Artificial Intelligence, 1977.

248 Unification

A process, used in **resolution** <204>, for determining whether two expressions of the **predicate calculus** <180> will match. Terms of an expression in predicate calculus may be of one of three forms: **constant**, **variable** or **function**, where the last of these is made up of a function symbol applied to a number of terms. A **substitution** is a set of ordered pairs where the first element of each pair is a term and the second a variable. Applying such a substitution to a formula means that each variable appearing in the set of ordered pairs is replaced by the term which it is matched with in the substitution. Two expressions are unifiable if there is a substitution (the unifier) which when applied to both expressions makes them identical. A unification algorithm determines whether the given expressions are unifiable and, if so, finds a unifying substitution. It is usual in **resolution** based systems to specify that the substitution which is applied to unify two expressions is the most general such substitution, thus the expressions lose as little generality as is necessary to make the resolution go through.

Contributor: Dave Plummer.

Reference

Nilsson, N.J. *Principles of Artificial Intelligence*, Tioga Pub. Co., Palo Alto, California, 1980.

249 Unification Grammars

Unification Grammar (UG) is the collective name for a group of linguistic formalisms and theories based on the idea of linguistic objects as partial information structures. The primary operation for combining such structures is **unification <248>**. Most UGs assume that linguistic objects are graph structures - sets of pairs of feature names and feature values, with the values possibly complex. However, grammar formalisms based on term unification, such as **Definite Clause Grammars <55>**, are closely allied, even though term and graph unification were introduced independently (by Robinson and Kay respectively). As well as providing a sound understanding of how features in the sense of traditional grammar should behave, UGs appear to offer great flexibility in their computational properties, due to the monotonic (order-independent) nature of the operation of unification. Current research issues in UGs include the definition of more expressive feature logics for describing linguistic objects, and efficient algorithms for computing with these.

Contributor: Pete Whitelock.

References

Gazdar, G., Klein, E., Pullum, G. and Sag, I. *Generalized Phrase Structure Grammar.* Basil Blackwell, Oxford, 1985.

Pereira, F.C.N. *Grammars and Logics of Partial Information.* SRI Technical Note 420, Menlo Park, California, 1987.

Shieber, S.M. *An Introduction to Unification-Based Approaches to Grammar.* CSLI Lecture Notes 4, Chicago University Press, 1986.

250 Universal Graph Representation

A method of storing and organising a database of graphs that reduces some expensive (exponential) operations to less expensive (linear) set operations. The universal graph is a graph that is a single "super" graph that contains all the graphs in the database as subgraphs. These subgraphs can be referenced as subsets of nodes in the universal graph. It is applicable to many applications requiring graph representation such as a **semantic net <213>**, chemical structures, networks, etc.

Contributor: Mohan Ahuja.

Reference

Levinson, R.A. Self-organising retrieval system for graphs. In *Proceedings of the AAAI*, pages 203–206. American Association for Artificial Intelligence, 1984.

251 Variable-valued Logic

Variable-valued logic is an extension of some known **many-valued logics** (MVL) in two directions:

1 It permits the propositions and variables in the propositions to take values from different domains, which can vary in the kind and number of elements and also in the structure relating to the elements.

2 It generalises some of the traditionally used operators and adds new operators which are 'most orthogonal' to the former.

Variable-valued logics have found applications in pattern recognition, medical **decision making**, discrimination of structural textures. These logics have been successfully used in construction of diagnostic expert systems that can acquire knowledge by **inductive learning** from examples.

Contributor: L.J. Kohout.

References

Michalski, R.S. Variable-valued logic and its application to pattern recognition and machine learning. In D.C. Rine, editor, *Computer Science and Multiple-Valued Logic: Theory and Applications*, North-Holland, Amsterdam and New York, 1977.

Michalski, R.S. and Chilansky, R.L. Knowledge acquisition by encoding expert rules versus computer induction from examples: a case study involving soya-bean pathology. In *Fuzzy Reasoning and its Applications*, Academic Press, London, 1981.

252 Viewer-centred Co-ordinates

Objects described in viewer-centred co-ordinates, as opposed to **object-centred co-ordinates <157>**, are those described in terms of a co-ordinate frame centred on the viewer, i.e. the viewer is considered to form the origin of the system and axes are defined relative to the line of sight and the retina. The representations of such objects must be transformed whenever the viewer moves.

Contributors: T P Pridmore, S R Pollard, S P Stenton.

Reference

Marr, D. *Vision: a computational investigaion into the human representation and processing of visual information.* W.H. Freeman, New York, 1982.

253 Viewpoint determination

Alias: model parameter determination

An important problem in model-based computer vision systems is to solve for the orientation and position of a three-dimensional object given some matches between features of the object and edges in the image. This algorithm provides a practical solution to the problem, including the difficult case of determining full three-dimensional viewpoint from locations of features in a two-dimensional image. The method is also capable of solving for internal model parameters such as variable sizes and articulations. The solution is based upon providing a rough initial estimate for the unknown parameters and then using Newton iteration to achieve an optimal least-squares fit. An important application is as part of a search process, in which a few matches can be used to determine viewpoint, which in turn constrains the locations of further matches.

Contributor: David Lowe.

Reference

Lowe, D.G. *Perceptual Organisation and Visual Recognition.* Kluwer Academic Publishers, Boston, Mass., 1985.

254 Viewsphere Representation

A method of object representation in which the appearance (under orthographic projection) of the object is modelled over the sphere of possible viewing directions. As the object's appearance in intensity terms depends on the illumination, the form of appearance usually modelled is more stable, *e.g.* the visibility of a region or the topology of a line drawing of the object. The representation may then consist of the viewsphere regions in which the appearance remains constant and the corresponding appearances in those regions. Considerable interest is also shown in the boundaries between viewsphere regions, which often represent singularities of appearance.

Contributor: R.M. Cameron-Jones

Reference

Gigus, Z., Canny, J. and Seidel, R. Efficiently computing and representing aspect graphs of polyhedral objects. *Second International Conference on Computer Vision*, pages 30–39, 1988.

255 Vocoder Representation

The **vocoder** representation characterises the speech signal in terms of energy in a series of fixed frequency bands. This form of analysis has been used as a stage in **speech recognition**, and as a means of data compression in storing speech for later **resynthesis**.

Contributor: Steve Isard.

256 Vowel Quadrilateral

Alias: **vowel analysis**.

Employs an 8-pole **linear predictive coding <128>** analysis to provide 9 vocal tract log area parameters which are mapped by a principal component transformation into a plane. The principal component coefficients are calculated off-line. Can provide a real-time display of vowel position; and a further rotational transformation gives close approximation to classical vowel quadrilateral.

Contributor: Geoff Bristow.

Reference

Bristow, F. and Fallside, G.J. Computer display of vowel quadrilateral with real-time representation of articulation. *Electronics Letters*, 14:107–109, 1978.

Index

N. J. Nilsson: Principles of Artificial Intelligence. XV, 476 pages, 139 figs., 1982

J. H. Siekmann, G. Wrightson (Eds.): Automation of Reasoning 1. Classical Papers on Computational Logic 1957–1966. XXII, 525 pages, 1983

J. H. Siekmann, G. Wrightson (Eds.): Automation of Reasoning 2. Classical Papers on Computational Logic 1967–1970. XXII, 638 pages, 1983

L. Bolc (Ed.): The Design of Interpreters, Compilers, and Editors for Augmented Transition Networks. XI, 214 pages, 72 figs., 1983

M. M. Botvinnik: Computers in Chess. Solving Inexact Search Problems. With contributions by A. I. Reznitsky, B. M. Stilman, M. A. Tsfasman, A. D. Yudin. Translated from the Russian by A. A. Brown. XIV, 158 pages, 48 figs., 1984

L. Bolc (Ed.): Natural Language Communication with Pictorial Information Systems. VII, 327 pages, 67 figs., 1984

R. S. Michalski, J. G. Carbonell, T. M. Mitchell (Eds.): Machine Learning. An Artificial Intelligence Approach. XI, 572 pages, 1984

C. Blume, W. Jakob: Programming Languages for Industrial Robots. XIII, 376 pages, 145 figs., 1986

J. W. Lloyd: Foundations of Logic Programming. Second, extended edition. XII, 212 pages, 1987

L. Bolc (Ed.): Computational Models of Learning. IX, 208 pages, 34 figs., 1987

L. Bolc (Ed.): Natural Language Parsing Systems. XVIII, 367 pages, 151 figs., 1987

N. Cercone, G. McCalla (Eds.): The Knowledge Frontier. Essays in the Representation of Knowledge. XXXV, 512 pages, 93 figs., 1987

G. Rayna: REDUCE. Software for Algebraic Computation. IX, 329 pages, 1987

D. D. McDonald, L. Bolc (Eds.): Natural Language Generation Systems. XI, 389 pages, 84 figs., 1988

L. Bolc, M. J. Coombs (Eds.): Expert System Applications. IX, 471 pages, 84 figs., 1988

Springer Series
SYMBOLIC COMPUTATION - *Artificial Intelligence*

C.-H. Tzeng: A Theory of Heuristic Information in Game-Tree Search. X, 107 pages, 22 figs., 1988

H. Coelho, J. C. Cotta: Prolog by Example. How to Learn, Teach and Use It. X, 382 pages, 68 figs., 1988

L. Kanal, V. Kumar (Eds.): Search in Artificial Intelligence. X, 482 pages, 67 figs., 1988

H. Abramson, V. Dahl: Logic Grammars. XIV, 234 pages, 40 figs., 1989

R. Hausser: Computation of Language. An Essay on Syntax, Semantics, and Pragmatics in Natural Man-Machine Communication. XVI, 425 pages, 1989

P. Besnard: An Introduction to Default Logic. XI, 201 pages, 1989

A. Kobsa, W. Wahlster (Eds.): User Models in Dialog Systems. XI, 471 pages, 113 figs., 1989

B. D'Ambrosio: Qualitative Process Theory Using Linguistic Variables. X, 156 pages, 22 figs., 1989

V. Kumar, P. S. Gopalakrishnan, L. N. Kanal (Eds.) Parallel Algorithms for Machine Intelligence and Vision. XI, 433 pages, 148 figs., 1990

Y. Peng, J. A. Reggia: Abductive Inference Models for Diagnostic Problem-Solving. XII, 284 pages, 25 figs., 1990

A. Bundy (Ed.): Catalogue of Artificial Intelligence Techniques. Third, revised edition. XV, 179 pages, 1990